BILINGUAL LITERACY DEVELOPMENT AT HOME

This book explores pedagogical implications for how children read, write, respond to literature, and begin to learn an additional language in the home context.

Using a longitudinal ethnographic study, it explores a bilingual child's literacy development over a span of four years from kindergarten to the third grade in a real-life home context in the United States. Written from a parent-researcher's perspective, it illustrates the child's Mandarin Chinese and English language support at home and in the community during the pandemic, and charts the development in bilingual reading and writing, multimodal reading responses to children's literature, and learning Spanish as a third language. Through rich and detailed descriptions, the case study methodology allows a clear articulation of the project's focus and foregrounds the exploration of reading as a sociopsycholinguistic process, as well as highlighting multimodality in reading and writing responses, translanguaging, and bilingual and bicultural identities to study and teach culturally and linguistically diverse children.

It will be a valuable resource for literacy researchers, scholars, and bilingual educators with interests in sociolinguistics, literacy education, bilingualism, and translanguaging.

Yang Wang 王杨 is Professor in Language and Literacy in the Department of Teacher Education at the University of South Carolina, U.S.A.

BILINGUAL LITERACY DEVELOPMENT AT HOME

A Longitudinal Ethnographic Exploration of Bilingual Reading and Writing

Yang Wang

Routledge
Taylor & Francis Group
NEW YORK AND LONDON

Designed cover image: © Yang Wang

First published 2026
by Routledge
605 Third Avenue, New York, NY 10158

and by Routledge
4 Park Square, Milton Park, Abingdon, Oxon, OX14 4RN

Routledge is an imprint of the Taylor & Francis Group, an informa business

ISBN: 978-1-032-85203-4 (hbk)
ISBN: 978-1-032-81258-8 (pbk)
ISBN: 978-1-003-51706-1 (ebk)

DOI: 10.4324/9781003517061

Typeset in Times New Roman
by codeMantra

This book is dedicated to my daughter, CoCo Li 李师杨—
my research participant, my inspiration, and
my best friend—as well as to all multilingual
children and their families.

CONTENTS

FIGURES AND TABLES

Figures

Tables

ACKNOWLEDGEMENTS

I extend my deepest gratitude to my daughter, Shiyang Carol Li (CoCo)—my research participant, my inspiration, and my best friend—and her father for being my most cherished research partners. I am especially grateful to CoCo's Lǎolao, Shujie Yang, and her Grandma Carol Gilles for the enduring love and support they have given to both CoCo and me. Their care has sustained us in more ways than words can express.

To CoCo's grandparents, uncles, aunts, and cousins in mainland China and England—thank you for being just a video call away and for nurturing the familial, cultural, and linguistic ties that remain central to our lives. To my dearest friends, who patiently listened to my reflections on bilingual parenting and the writing process through countless messages and early morning phone calls, thank you for your steadfast encouragement and care. I am also thankful for the family friends who shared our pandemic bubble and helped create the stories and memories woven throughout this research.

I owe special thanks to my mentors, Dr. Carol Gilles and Dr. Lucy Spence, whose belief in this project never wavered. Your mentorship, insightful feedback, and constant encouragement helped bring this book to life. You planted the seed for this work and walked with me through each stage of its growth.

I am also grateful to my colleagues at the University of South Carolina for their generosity of spirit and thoughtful insights. My sincere thanks go to academic friends Dr. Sally Brown, Dr. Tasha Laman, and Dr. Rong Zhang for reading early drafts of chapters and offering invaluable feedback. Thanks to Dr. Ling Hao for inviting CoCo and me to the family book club, co-drafting chapter 4 with me, and thoughtfully reviewing my drafts.

To my doctoral students, Julie Stensland and Shuang Du—thank you for your assistance with data analysis in chapters 2 and 5. I am also thankful to Jing Zhang and Celina-Maria Espinosa for reading and responding to my drafts, and to many others who listened and offered support along the way.

Finally, heartfelt thanks to Ariel Robinson—my friend and editor—for her thoughtful reading and questions that strengthened this manuscript, and to the editorial team at Routledge for their guidance and support throughout the publication process. I sincerely thank all my readers of this book for your interest in and dedication to bilingual education.

1

INTRODUCTION

When I asked my daughter, CoCo Li, a seven-and-a-half-year-old bilingual child, to illustrate what being bilingual meant to her, she created a self-portrait as a gingerbread girl (see Figure 1.1). Through this drawing, CoCo depicted her multifaceted linguistic and cultural identities.

CoCo incorporated multilingual texts beyond direct translations using English, Chinese, and Spanish to describe herself (see Figure 1.2). She placed the Chinese characters "中文 [Chinese]" on her mouth and "English" on her tongue, symbolizing her ability to speak both languages. On the left leg, she wrote "learning Spanish, Espanile [Español]," demonstrating her emerging trilingualism. Throughout this book, all texts within quotation marks in this book reflect CoCo's original language use and spelling, while English translations are provided in brackets.

CoCo also embedded cultural symbols in her illustration. She used the Chinese character "福" for the nose and on the head bow. She marked its meaning with arrows, "means luck" as a "sybole [symbol] of luck in Chinese" to explain its significance. On her forehead, CoCo inscribed "王" explaining that it is the "sybole [symbol] of power in Chinese." She introduced her English name on two buttons and her Chinese name on her right leg. She also embedded pictures and symbols within her figure. In her hands, CoCo drew her favorite Chinese food—a dumpling and a steamed bun. Additionally, she illustrated aspects of her personality and interests: she wrote "I am always happy" next to a smiley face, "I am kind" with an image of herself helping me, and "I am funny" besides a drawing of her telling me a joke. She also shared personal aspirations and family details, including "want to be a teacher," "love music," "like reading," "losing a toth [tooth]," "My dad is a sintiest [scientist]," and "My mom is a

DOI: 10.4324/9781003517061-1

FIGURE 1.1 CoCo Drawing her Gingerbread Girl

FIGURE 1.2 CoCo's Gingerbread Girl

teacher." CoCo illustrated all her texts in her portrait. Through this drawing, she represents herself as a multilingual speaker, highlighting her use of languages, cultural components, personal identity, family connections, and things that are important to her.

Context and Scope of This Book

According to the United States Census Bureau (n.d.), 67.8 million people five years and older—22% of the U.S. population—used a language other than English at home in 2019 (Dietrich & Hernandez, 2022). The four major language groups in the United States include Spanish, other Indo-European languages, Asian and Pacific Island languages, and various other languages. In our home state, 7.5% of residents reported speaking a language other than English at home (Dietrich & Hernandez, 2022). Despite this linguistic diversity, developing bilingual literacy in a predominantly monolingual environment presents significant challenges in multiple dimensions.

Persistent misconceptions about bilingualism further complicate the process of raising bilingual children. These include myths such as the belief that children should first master their first language (L1) proficiency before learning a second language (L2), that bilingual individuals have only partial proficiency in each language, and that code-mixing indicates linguistic confusion rather than a strategic use of linguistic resources (Baker, 2014; Crisfield, 2021). How do bilingual children interrogate those language hierarchies to develop bilingual literacy? Additionally, all students were negatively impacted by the COVID-19 pandemic (Baker & Wright, 2021), and the impact on bilingual speakers was even more significant. Many minoritized communities suffered from inequalities, high infection, and death rates. While interrupted school was challenging for all students, bilingual children lacked learning resources in online instruction (Baker & Wright, 2021).

This book documents a bilingual child, CoCo, who developed her biliteracy in two languages, English and Mandarin Chinese, over four years from kindergarten through third grade in a U.S. home context from a parent-researcher's perspective. This book presents CoCo's reading and writing development, multimodal reading responses to culturally relevant children's literature, and early engagement with Spanish as a third language. To better understand biliteracy development, the following key themes frame this work:

- **Bilingual Reading Development:** CoCo's home language of Mandarin and English language reading development journey demonstrates that reading is a sociopsycholinguistic process. She utilized her full linguistic repertoire for comprehension. Her reading views and identities were fluid and greatly influenced by both parental and instructional contexts.

- **Home-Based Writing Practices**: Through daily journal writing, CoCo developed bilingual writing skills, built her confidence in writing, used her full linguistic repertoire and modes in writing, and formed her bilingual identity. Her parents' scaffolding played a crucial role in this process (Wood et al., 1976).
- **Family and Community Engagement:** A virtual, community-based family reading workshop provided a space for CoCo to discuss culturally relevant literature books with the parent-researcher and to respond in multimodal ways. CoCo developed bicultural identities through cultural discussions at home, the process of creating multimodal products, and sharing with other families from similar linguistic and cultural backgrounds.
- **Trilingual Language Acquisition:** While developing biliteracy in Mandarin and English, CoCo also explored Spanish as a third language (L3). In her discourses and responses to Spanish picture books, she showed different purposes for using these three languages and transferred between Mandarin and English to make sense of Spanish texts.
- **Identity Formation:** CoCo, an emergent bilingual child, constructed her bilingual and bicultural identities through varied literacy practices at home and social interactions.

This study describes the simultaneous acquisition of bilingualism (Baker & Wright, 2021) and examines the hierarchies between two languages and between school and family supports. The objectives are to provide researchers with insights gained from the biliteracy development process, offer educators strategies for strengthening home-school partnerships, and equip parents with resources for raising bilingual and trilingual children. The findings suggest implications for ongoing discussions on biliteracy research and will help all stakeholders bridge these language differences and help emergent bilinguals achieve academic success.

This first chapter outlines the purpose of this book, the overall theoretical support for each chapter, the participant, the context, the research method, and chapter previews. Subsequent sections introduce the Mandarin Chinese language and literacy and the theoretical support, including reading as a sociopsycholinguistic process, reader-response theory, translanguaging, multimodality, and identities.

Chinese Language and Literacy

Mandarin Chinese is the standard modern form of the Chinese language and serves as the official national language of Mainland China. Despite the existence of eight major regional dialects in Mainland China, these linguistic varieties share a common written language (Shei, 2014). The Chinese language belongs to the Sino-Tibetan language family and employs a logographic writing system, wherein each Chinese character represents a syllable and a unit of meaning—morphemic (Goodman et al., 2012; Li et al., 2022). Some scholars maintain that Chinese is logographic—the characters represent words, while some insist that it is ideographic—the characters convey ideas. In the written language, Chinese characters represent meaning, and many represent both meaning and sound. Chinese characters are generally classified into six categories (Shei, 2014):

- Pictograms 象形字: Simplified pictures of material objects, e.g., 日 (rì—Chinese pinyin, sun—English meaning), 目 (mù, eye).
- Ideograms 指事字: Direct iconic illustration, e.g., 上 (shàng, up) pointing up means up, and 下 (xià, down) pointing down means down.
- Ideogrammic compounds 会意字: A combination of two or more pictographic or ideographic characters to indicate a third meaning, e.g., 泪 (lèi, tear) depicting water from an eye, 从 (cóng, follow) representing one person is following the other, and 众 (zhòng, group) representing a group of people.
- Phono-semantic compounds 形声字: A combination of the semantic component (general meaning) and the phonetic component (pronunciation), which are the most numerous characters. For example, within the compound character 骑 (qí, riding), the left part 马 (mǎ, horse) conveys the meaning, and the right part 奇 (qí, odd) suggests its sound.
- Rebus 假借字: Borrowing or phonetic loan from complex characters.
- Transformed cognates 转注字: Meaning influenced by others, the smallest category.

The fundamental semantic unit in Chinese is a word that is typically composed of two or more Chinese characters. Characters with basic meanings can form Chinese words, and most words consist of two or more characters (Pan & Feng, 2017). Consequently, readers of Chinese must pay more attention to larger units of language, such as words or phrases, rather than isolated characters (Pan & Feng, 2017).

Chinese pinyin is the phonetic system for pronouncing Chinese characters. Pinyin letters make use of the Latin alphabet, with one additional letter, "ü" (Wang & Andrews, 2021). Due to the differences between Chinese and English phonology, certain English phonemes lack direct Chinese equivalents. Some phonemes look alike but are not equivalent in pronunciation. Furthermore, Chinese is monosyllabic. That means the initial consonant and a vowel often make one syllable. Some vowels stand as one syllable. While English is monotone, the Chinese language has four distinct tones: the first tone (high level, -), the second tone (rising, /), the third tone (falling-rising, v), and the fourth tone (falling, \). A single syllable may correspond to multiple characters with distinct meanings, resulting in a high frequency of homophones. Chinese dictionaries typically contain over 3,000 homophones (Wang & Andrews, 2021).

Chinese syntax generally follows a subject-verb or subject-verb-object formula (Shei, 2014). However, compared to English, there are not many grammar rules in Chinese syntactic structure; for example, subject-verb agreement or marked plurality (Wang & Yang, 2007). Past and future tenses are marked with additional characters. Another key distinction is the absence of spaces between words in the Chinese writing system, which can pose challenges for early readers.

In Mainland China, children learn to read and write simplified Chinese characters in the first grade (MOE of P.R.C., 2022). They start learning Chinese characters from the visuals, pictograms, and ideograms, for instance, 日 (rì, sun), 月 (yuè, moon), 水 (shuǐ, water), and 火 (huǒ, fire). They learn the strokes of writing characters and the structure of characters by practice and drill. Children learn to read simple texts (e.g., nursery rhymes, poems, and songs) following reading aloud, choral reading, repetition, and recitation. By the end of the first quarter of first grade, children are introduced to pinyin—a phonetic system that uses letters in the Latin alphabet and four different tone marks to spell out Chinese sounds. Textbooks, anthologies, and early children's literature books include pinyin alongside Chinese written characters, enabling children to sound out the words after learning pinyin.

Children are expected to learn approximately 300 new characters in first grade, 500 new characters in second grade, and another 500 characters in third grade (MOE of P.R.C., 2022). In addition, they learn to identify more characters in context. From the second semester of second grade, the written texts do not print with pinyin in the textbooks except for some newly introduced or complex characters. Children are expected to read Chinese characters independently without pinyin support in the third grade. Literature books for the upper elementary level are typically printed solely in Chinese characters without pinyin.

Theoretical Support

Reader Response Theory

Rosenblatt (1978/1994) conceived that reading is a continuous transaction among the reader, text, and context to create understanding. Readers' stances or purposes for reading guide their understanding. Efferent reading focuses primarily on the public aspects of sense and involves "analyzing, abstracting, and accumulating what will be retained after the reading," while aesthetic reading intensifies the private aspects of sense and focuses on "experiencing what is being evoked, lived through, during the reading" (Rosenblatt, 1978/1994, p. 184). Those two stances are not in opposition but shift on a continuum throughout the reading event. Readers need to decide what stance to adopt, and children should be able to shift their stances between efferent and aesthetic (Rosenblatt,

2005b). Effective readers make purposeful transactions with the texts (Paugh & MacPhee, 2023; Rosenblatt, 2018).

Bilingual children often apply their funds of knowledge—cultural resources, cultural knowledge, and life experiences (González et al., 2005; Moll, 2014) in their reading. Reader response theory informed analyses in Chapters 2, 4, and 5 for examining CoCo's reading responses to multi-genre texts, culturally relevant literature books, and texts in her first, second, and third languages.

Reading as a Sociopsycholinguistic Process

Reading is a transactional sociopsycholinguistic process (Goodman, 2014). Readers utilize all language systems to make meaning from the text (Goodman et al., 2016; Weaver, 2002). Linguistic systems—including graphophonics, syntax, and semantics, and pragmatic systems—context, prior knowledge, and culture, constitute language systems (Watson et al., 1988). Culture influences all other cueing systems, and language exists within a sociocultural context (Goodman et al., 2005). In the sociopsycholinguistic process, readers construct meaning from the text through cognitive strategies: initiating reading, sampling, and selecting from the text; making predictions and inferences; confirming or disconfirming predictions; integrating meaning; and terminating their reading (Goodman, 2014).

When readers' observed responses vary from their expected responses, it is called a miscue (Goodman et al., 2005). Listening and observing readers' reading provides us with a "window on the reading process" (Goodman, 1973, p. 5). Comprehension is the end product of reading, while the comprehending process, in which readers are engaged, is dynamic (Goodman, 2014). To be more specific, Goodman et al. (2016) stated that readers mentally create their texts for understanding as they encounter the authors' texts; readers' perceptions of the authors' texts are more salient than the texts; what readers think they see is more crucial than what they actually see in the texts. Ken Goodman (1973) developed miscue analysis for observing reading behavior and analyzing the reading process. Yetta Goodman, Dorothy Watson, and Carolyn Burke (2005) later expanded this to a modified miscue analysis and refined it for classroom teachers and researchers. They created a classroom procedure, an informal procedure, and an in-depth procedure for documenting children's reading practices. The in-depth procedure was adopted in Chapter 2 to analyze CoCo's bilingual reading process. Equally important, miscue analysis is a culturally relevant assessment tool for bilingual readers because it values their languages and sociocultural backgrounds (Kabuto, 2017).

Retrospective miscue analysis (RMA) is an "after reading" conversation between the reader and the researcher/teacher about the reader's miscues (Goodman et al., 2014; Moore & Gilles, 2005), which was also adopted in

Chapter 2. RMA helps readers view their reading processes, become aware of and obtain greater control of their reading strategies, and construct meaning using their language knowledge (Moore & Gilles, 2005). RMA, as an assessment and instructional tool, helps teachers understand readers' reading views and strategy use, and it provides insights into the reading process (Moore & Gilles, 2005). Kabuto (2022) further expanded miscue analysis as a culturally relevant reading assessment practice for bilingual learners. This procedure includes four major components: a reading interview in each language, oral reading in each language, retelling in the language of the reader's choice, and reflective dialogue on reading. Espinosa and Ascenzi-Moreno (2021) also tailored miscue analysis for teachers working with emergent bilinguals.

Multimodality

From the social semiotic perspective, meaning is made through various modes, including all signs of words, pictures, gestures, music, and so on (Kress, 2010; Siegel, 2006). Modes are means or different mediums to create meaning, and meaning moves across modes (Cowan & Kress, 2017). Meaning-making within a mode is transformation, for instance, a text change from one genre to another, while meaning transfer across modes is transduction, for instance, from speech to image (Cowan & Kress, 2017; Kress, 2010). Multimodal texts include texts in more than one mode for representation (Serafini, 2015). Multimodal literacy refers to the use of diverse modes for meaning construction (Jewitt, 2008; Kress, 2010). "All meaning-making is multimodal" (New London Group, 1996, p. 81) and requires designing (Cowan & Kress, 2017).

Prior research has employed multimodal approaches to study young emergent bilinguals globally (Brown & Hao, 2022). In fact, the act of writing is a multimodal practice (Kenner, 2003). Chapters 3, 4, and 5 draw upon multimodality to explore CoCo's meaning-making after discussing culturally relevant picture books, reading books in a third language, and representing herself in journal writing.

Translanguaging

Bilingual learners use their full linguistic repertoire in meaning-making (García & Li, 2014). Translanguaging affirms that there is one linguistic system. Canagarajah (2011) defines translanguaging as "the ability of multilingual speakers to shuttle between languages, treating the diverse languages that form their repertoire as an integrated system" (p. 401). Multilingual minds do not function as two separate monolinguals operating independently (Franck et al., 2024). Translanguaging happens spontaneously and pragmatically (Baker, 2014). The purposes can be to assist and motivate learning, gain greater metalinguistic awareness, affirm bilingual identities, interact and communicate socially, and empower (García, 2017). Additionally, bilinguals use translanguaging to emphasize a particular point, substitute when a person does not know a word, express concepts without equivalences, solve problems, reinforce, clarify, express identity, report speech, interject into a conversation, ease tension, change attitude or relationship, exclude, change in topic, and imitate (Baker & Wright, 2021). Multilingualism influences various domains of creativity, self-regulation, social skills, and music skills besides language skills (Franck et al., 2024).

Translanguaging is not only a natural way for bilingual children to construct meaning but also a transformative pedagogy that can be applied in language classrooms and Science, Technology, Engineering, and Mathematics (STEM) classrooms (García & Li, 2014). Educators (Espinosa & Ascenzi-Moreno, 2021; Fu et al., 2019; Li, 2014) have adopted translanguaging in teaching literacy to emergent bilingual learners and to leverage children's home language practices to develop their school languages. Wei Li (2014) also discussed a co-learning model between teachers and students in which all knowledge is valued, all sharers are valued and care for each other, and all learn from one another. This kind of co-learning environment shares power among the learners, situates learning in the real world and community, and empowers collective and individual meaning-making and identity exploration (Li, 2014). Multilingual interactions are often aided by multimodalities, and translanguaging includes all meaning-making modes (García & Li, 2014). Chapters 2, 3, 4, and 5 employed translanguaging as a lens to showcase CoCo's multilingual literacy development.

Identity

Identity is not static but always changing. Identities are created and confined in a sociocultural context (Norton, 2013; 2018). Bilinguals enact multiple identities and have different identities in different contexts. They may have conflicts of identities and construct and reconstruct identities (Baker & Wright, 2021). When acquiring a second language, inculcation into a culture and change in identity occur along with it (Baker & Wright, 2021). The identity formation process is ongoing, constantly constructed, and a process of negotiation (Wang, 2008).

Bilingual families may perceive heritage language differently, from essential, emotional, pragmatic to peripheral, and their perceptions influence their investment (Little, 2020). Learning bilingual children's identities helps educators understand their literacy practices and refine instructions and assessments (Kabuto, 2010, 2022). Chapters 2, 3, 4, and 5 document CoCo's lived-through experiences of constructing her linguistic identities, sociocultural identities, and transnational and ethnic-racial identities.

Methodology

This qualitative longitudinal ethnographic case study (Compton-Lilly, 2021; Creswell & Creswell, 2018; Merriam, 2009) describes CoCo's biliteracy development over a span of four years, from kindergarten to the third grade (five to eight years old), in a real-life home context in the United States. As a qualitative case study (Stake, 1995), this research focuses on a single bounded case: the biliteracy development of my daughter, CoCo. I selected my only child as the sole participant in this study. The ethnographic case study approach allows for a clear articulation of the research focus, a rich and detailed description, and an emphasis on semiotic processes in a sociocultural context (Compton-Lilly, 2021). While this study centers on an individual case, the prolonged timeframe, extensive data collection through face-to-face and virtual modalities, and the use of thick descriptions contribute meaningfully to the existing knowledge in the field on biliteracy development.

Researcher Positionality

As a parent-researcher (Kabuto & Martens, 2014), I provided an emic perspective and collected rich kidwatching data (Goodman & Owocki, 2002) because the participant and I lived together, and I knew the context well. Therefore, I collected rich observation data that showed CoCo's language and literacy development, language deviation, salient moments, and critical incidents. The parental and professional perspectives gave me the privilege of telling the story. As a literacy professor with proficiency in both English and Mandarin Chinese, I provided a linguistic and cultural insider's perspective. Recognizing that I needed to be critical if I wanted to understand bilingual children's learning experiences, I discussed the critical moments with my literacy colleagues and research assistants to ensure ethical consideration and invited them to review selected data and manuscript chapters.

I was born and raised in Mainland China. I began learning English as a foreign language after I developed my L1 proficiency at elementary school. My early exposure to English consisted of learning English letters and some words from my eldest cousin and an English language learning television program for children. One of my parents' friends gave me a set of English textbooks and cassettes along with them that were used for that television program, which was broadcast every weekday night for about 30 minutes. My formal English education began in middle school, where I studied English through daily 45-minute lessons. Students purchased one required textbook each semester and multiple workbooks and composition books. I remember reading after the teacher and the cassette player in class to practice oral language. There were no other reading texts or extracurricular materials available. Then, high school English education continued in a similar format, with increased emphasis on preparing for high-stakes examinations. I later studied English Education for four years in college. After obtaining my Bachelor of Arts, I worked as a foreign language instructor at a university for four years, where I taught required English language courses to undergraduate students and Chinese language courses to international students. My academic journey then led me to the United States, where I earned a master's degree in Teaching English to Speakers of Other Languages (TESOL) and a doctoral degree in literacy.

As a faculty member in Language and Literacy for over a decade, my interest in early literacy and emergent biliteracy development deepened with the birth of my child. Inspired by the children's literacy development research from Prisca Martens (1996) and Bobbie Kabuto (2010), I began closely observing my own child's language development. Through this case study, I aim to share my findings with literacy educators, teachers, parents, and community members who work with emergent bilingual children.

The Participant

CoCo was born and grew up in a southeastern city in the United States, where 91.82% of the residents are monolingual English speakers. The largest non-English-speaking group is Latinx, approximately 3.84% of the population, and Asian or Pacific Islander residents make up approximately 1.9% of the population (Columbia Population, 2025). Although our zoned school district has a world language program, it is the only district in this area without a language immersion program. CoCo's father shares a similar English learning experience with me, and obtained his medical degree and PhD in medicine in Mainland China prior to his postdoctoral fellowship and research associate position in the United States. Mandarin Chinese is the primary language spoken at home, while English is the dominant language in CoCo's school environment. She acquires Chinese and English simultaneously.

Schooling

At ten months old, CoCo enrolled in a full-day English-speaking daycare near our home. Before turning two years old, she transitioned to a university-affiliated children's center, about 30 minutes from our house. That preschool maintained a close partnership with the university. University student athletes visited to read books aloud to children regularly, physical education pre-service teachers led weekly physical activities, and music education pre-service teachers sang and danced with the children once a week. The children also participated in collaborative programs with the local library and other educational programs.

The preschool had a diverse student population. There was one mixed-race boy in her two-year-old room, one Asian American boy and one mixed-race boy in the three-year-old room, and two Asian American and two mixed-race children in the 4K room. In the 4K room, CoCo spoke some Chinese with the other Chinese American girl. I volunteered to read Chinese American picture books to the group. Another girl's mother and grandma came to the class to share Indian culture. The lead teacher taught some Spanish and was open to different cultures. She even taught the children to play African American drums.

Then, CoCo attended a Mandarin Chinese immersion charter school for kindergarten at 4:11 (indicating four years and 11 months old). At that bilingual school, she received half-day instruction in Mandarin Chinese and half-day instruction in English. However, she only had full-day in-person experiences for five months before the COVID-19 pandemic. During that time, the school shifted to online asynchronous learning for the rest of her kindergarten. Afterward, she enrolled in a virtual full-day English program in our zoned school district for her first and second grades and returned to an English-only school for third grade.

Home Language Environment

Mandarin Chinese is the primary language spoken at home. My husband and I, as well as all extended family members, communicate in Mandarin. Some family members spoke a northeastern dialect of Mainland China. We have had story time since CoCo was born. Initially, I read board books to her in English and supplemented with Chinese translations due to a limited availability of Chinese books. As she grew older, I read Chinese books to CoCo before she went to bed. We switched to English read-alouds on weekends and on the days when she did not attend school. The purpose was to ensure that she could have balanced language input in both English and Chinese every day. When we commuted daily for over an hour to the university preschool and bilingual immersion school, we reinforced Chinese language learning by reading books, listening to read-alouds and Chinese songs, making phone calls, and talking in Chinese as much as we could in the car. CoCo's father and I took her to a variety of activities on weekends so she could have exposure to the English language environment: library story time, museum events, local events (e.g., state fair, international festival), playdates, birthday parties, grocery shopping, retail shopping, and day trips. The COVID-19 pandemic significantly restricted us from attending many in-person events. With more than two years of virtual learning, she only had a few friends to play with, primarily the children of my colleagues and friends, due to the pandemic's restrictions.

I started curating a personal library for CoCo when she was little. I purchased and received many books as gifts from my mentor, friends, and colleagues. CoCo had a large collection of Chinese books, including fictional stories, historical stories, fairytales, poems, fables, graphic novels, biographies, nonfiction books, magazines, etc. I bought these books when we visited China, and some were gifted by my friends. CoCo's book collection included board books, interactive books, and picture books in English in her first year. I also checked out some board books and pop-up books to read to her from the local public library. Then I brought some books in Chinese for her from China whenever we visited. I went to bookstores wherever we made a stop to visit our family and friends. In the stores, many books for children were collections of worksheets, history books, and books of ancient poems and essays. Many picture books were about similar historical topics or were translated from international literature. Authentic contemporary picture books were rare. I also asked friends to order books online in China and asked my mother or friends to help bring those books when they visited us. Occasionally, I purchased Chinese books online. Figure 1.3 shows CoCo's bookcase when she was five years old. Our book collection include:

- **Chinese books**: Authentic contemporary realistic fiction written and illustrated by Chinese authors and illustrators, literature books translated from other countries, traditional Chinese folklore, nonfiction books, anthologies, language arts textbooks used in Mainland China, and magazines.
- **Bilingual books in Chinese and English**: Chinese folklore, nonfiction books about Chinese holidays, and bilingual dictionaries.
- **English books**: Picture books, chapter books, nonfiction books, graphic novels, and books about Asian American and Chinese American culture.
- **Spanish books**: Bilingual Spanish-English books and Spanish picture books.

Learning a heritage language in a non-heritage cultural context was challenging because it was impossible to replicate the heritage cultural experiences (Wang, 2008). A previous parent researcher, Xiao-Lei Wang (2008), called it a "second-hand language acquisition phenomenon" (p. 24). Therefore, I intentionally created more opportunities for CoCo to acquire her heritage language. For example, we celebrated all traditional heritage holidays in our home or with other families who share the same language, talked to our extended family members online, provided a print rich environment at home, encouraged and monitored her language input and output, and traveled to China to visit relatives and friends. CoCo documented those in her journals in Chapter 3. Additionally, Figure 1.4 shows CoCo playing mahjong with lǎolao (grandma) online. CoCo learned this traditional Chinese board game and talked to her lǎolao in Chinese. There was a Sunday Chinese language school and many options for virtual lessons through different platforms and companies. However, I opted to teach CoCo Chinese personally due to convenience and her specific learning needs. Accordingly, our family language policy (Cunningham, 2020; Macalister, 2017) was to use Chinese at home when we talked to each other. We used both Chinese and English during weekends, no school days, holidays, and summer and

FIGURE 1.3 CoCo's Bookcase (5:11)

FIGURE 1.4 CoCo Playing Mahjong with Lǎolao

winter breaks when CoCo was not exposed to the English language-dominant environment.

Data Collection

This qualitative longitudinal ethnographic case study provides a thick description of a bilingual child's literacy development. Very few researchers have had the opportunity to follow children's literacy journeys over an extended period. Just as Wang (2008), Kabuto (2010), and other parent-researchers (Kabuto & Martens, 2014), I collected rich kidwatching data from close observation (Goodman, 1978). The data collection includes reading recordings, discussion recordings, observation notes, interviews, writing pieces, and artifacts.

- **Audio recordings**: CoCo reading books in English and in Chinese, discussing those books, and reading Spanish picturebooks.
- **Video recordings**: CoCo using different languages when she interacted with reading and writing, reading her own writing pieces, talking about her writing and artwork, and presenting her work to family members and others.
- **Observation notes**: My notes capturing CoCo's language use.
- **Journals**: CoCo's journal writing entries from ages 5:1 to 8:7 (2019 to 2023).
- **Multimodal artifacts**: CoCo's multimodal work that she created in response to picturebooks in a virtual family book club.
- **Interviews**: CoCo's reading views, strategy use, language use, and literacy development.

Chapters 2, 3, 4, and 5 elaborate on the detailed data collection and analysis methods corresponding to each chapter's objectives. I will present a preview of each chapter below.

Chapter Previews

Chapter 2: Developing Bilingual Literacies: Reading in English and in Mandarin Chinese describes CoCo's reading development in English and Mandarin Chinese. Based on the lens of sociopsycholinguistic process of reading, this chapter highlights the simultaneous emergent bilingual literacy development of using language systems, linguistic repertoire, and translanguaging when CoCo reads researcher-selected English and Chinese print texts. The data collected include two or more reading sessions in each language from each grade level, observation notes, retrospective conversations on reading miscues and comprehension, and interviews. CoCo's reading miscues were marked and analyzed using the Reading Miscue Inventory In-depth Procedure (Goodman et al., 2005). The retellings, retrospective conversations (Goodman et al., 2014;

Moore & Gilles, 2005), interviews, and observation notes were open-coded, and codes were grouped for themes (Creswell & Creswell, 2018; Stake, 1995). The findings reveal that CoCo developed bilingual literacy simultaneously using all her language systems. She relied on the graphic and phonic systems and used all visual information for meaning-making in both languages. She employed her full linguistic repertoire and created her hidden connectors using a mesh of two languages when she encountered new words. Notably, CoCo's English reading strategy use evolved under the influence of school instruction from each of her grade levels, which was a shift from reliance on context and picture clues in early grades to a focus on word-level accuracy by third grade. CoCo's Chinese reading, in contrast, showcased her active predicting and questioning, and the impact of her dominant school instructional language. The findings suggest insights for biliteracy research to help all stakeholders bridge these language differences and help emergent bilinguals achieve academic success.

Chapter 3: A Thousand Days of Journaling: A Multilingual, Multimodal, Multigenre Home Writing Practice presents CoCo's writing development through her home journal writing practice from kindergarten to third grade. The dataset consists of 1,030 consecutive journal pieces written from December 2019 to May 2023. Using open descriptive coding (Miles et al., 2020), emergent themes included writing development, language use, modes of expression, and cultural connections. The findings illustrate that CoCo developed her writing skills and gradually took ownership of her writing, progressing from a narrator to a writer and, ultimately, to an author. CoCo's journal topics reflected her lived experiences, and her reading interests impacted her creation of various genres. While the primary goal of journaling was to reinforce her heritage language, she utilized her full linguistic repertoire (García & Li, 2014), which meant she mixed Chinese and English in her writing and added Spanish, her third language, in her journals. Additionally, she employed multimodal elements, such as illustrating the text, designing different text features, and borrowing mixed media in her journal. CoCo's journals serve as a rich record of her engagement with learning the cultural heritage living in a multicultural context, and maintaining transnational relationships. Through the sustained journaling practice, she not only developed her linguistic and traditional and multimodal writing skills but also formed her identities as a writer, author, multilingual speaker, and global citizen. This chapter underscores the significance of home writing practice for fostering authorship, multilingual development, and multicultural identity formation.

Chapter 4: Books, Discussions, and Artifacts: Reading and Responding to Bilingual and Bicultural Children's Literature Books illustrates CoCo's bilingual and bicultural development within in a year-long community-based virtual bilingual family book club. CoCo and I, as a dyad, read and discussed 28 culturally relevant picture books (Ladson-Billings, 2021) with a few other Chinese American families via a virtual live conferencing platform on a weekly basis during the COVID-19 pandemic in 2021. The book club met for a total of 18 sessions in the spring when CoCo was in first grade and ten sessions in the fall when she was in second grade. All sessions were recorded using this online conferencing platform. The discussions between the two of us were audio recorded and transcribed. All the artifacts created during these sessions were also collected for analysis. Employing reader response theory (Rosenblatt, 1978/1994) and multimodality (Jewitt, 2008; Kress, 2011), this chapter describes CoCo's evolving engagement with the literature books. Initially, she focused on retelling the main ideas and making personal connections, but over time, she progressed to asking questions, comparing the differences between fiction and real-life experiences, and creating projects inspired by the readings and discussions. Her artifacts reveal how she used the books as mentor texts, extended the book content with her lived experiences, blended Chinese and American cultural elements, and employed multiple modes of representation. The conversations between us helped CoCo resolve any uncertainties about her cultures and embrace her bicultural identity. The findings highlight how literature books serve as a window and a mirror for children to engage with their cultural heritage and as a sliding door for understanding mixed identities (Bishop, 1990). Parents played a pivotal role in expanding their children's funds of knowledge and fostering bilingual identities (Hao, 2023; Yang et al., 2021). Additionally, transgenerational relationships in the literature books and in real life strengthened CoCo's transnational connections and cultural understanding. Learning and maintaining the heritage language and culture were challenging and took time for the family. This chapter also offers recommendations for culturally relevant children's literature books and diverse response strategies. It emphasizes the importance of communication and collaboration between educators, researchers, and parents in supporting young children's bilingual and bicultural development.

Chapter 5: "好! Fine! ¡Perfecto!": From Being Bilingual to Becoming Trilingual explores CoCo's experiences of learning Spanish as her third language in a predominantly monolingual English-speaking environment in the southeastern United States. When she was seven years old and in the spring semester of second grade, CoCo read Spanish picture books in six reading sessions. The purpose was to understand how CoCo responded to Spanish texts and how she used her full linguistic repertoire to learn a third language. All picture books were either printed in Spanish only or in both Spanish and English. After reading, CoCo created her written responses about what she learned. Data sources include transcribed conversations in each session, written responses, observation notes, and a final interview. The findings reveal that CoCo actively identified similarities and differences across the three languages that she used. She purposefully selected different languages in her speech and products. She employed translanguaging in her discussions and writing to learn new vocabulary, indicate meaning, and transfer sound, syntax, and special marks across languages. Overall, the reading sessions provided a dynamic space for CoCo's trilingual development and ways of knowing (García et al., 2017). The language environment and communication purpose highly impacted CoCo's language use. Furthermore, this chapter discusses how translanguaging helped this emergent trilingual learner to navigate her learning of a new language using her full linguistic repertoire. Additionally, it highlights that translanguaging and multimodality supported her in forming trilingual identities and building her cultural understanding. These findings offer insights into how translanguaging and multimodality can facilitate emergent trilingualism and cultural integration.

Chapter 6: Concluding Thoughts synthesizes the findings of this book and provides a comprehensive analysis of CoCo's bilingual, trilingual, bicultural, and tricultural development in relation to the theoretical frameworks outlined in Chapter 1. This chapter situates this study within broader research contexts, highlighting its contribution to existing scholarship. This project expands the understanding of biliteracy development (Kabuto, 2010; 2022) and offers an in-depth case of a Chinese-English bilingual speaker acquiring Spanish as an additional language. This longitudinal ethnographic case study presents a more detailed description with multiple data collected in the home context about bilingual and trilingual development. My emic perspective as both a researcher and parent enhances the depth of analysis and contributes to showcasing CoCo's evolving literacy development and identity formation. This chapter also outlines key implications for researchers, educators, and community members, emphasizing the importance of leveraging home resources to support bilingual and trilingual development. Following the conclusion, CoCo shares her personal reflections on language learning after reading the draft of this book, offering her own perspective on her multilingual journey documented in this study.

Significance

The current literature in the literacy and bilingualism field primarily focuses on Spanish-English bilingual speakers in the United States, multilingual speakers of alphabetical languages in Europe, and English as a foreign language in Asian countries. The longitudinal studies have often been conducted by parent-researchers. For instance, Kabuto (2010) studied her daughter's biliteracy development in English and Japanese from three to seven years old, Martens (1996) documented her adopted daughter's monolingual literacy development from two to five, and Wang (2008) chronicled the stories of her two children acquiring English and two heritage languages, Chinese and French, from birth to 11.

This book presents the first longitudinal ethnographic case study to describe a Mandarin-Chinese and English bilingual child's literacy development within a home setting in the United States. Spanning over four years, it offers an in-depth exploration of CoCo's bilingual and trilingual literacy development with rich kidwatching (Goodman & Owocki, 2002) data, including audio and video recordings, interviews, observation notes, writing samples, and artifacts. Notably, much of this data was collected during the COVID-19 pandemic, providing valuable insights into family literacy development during this unique time, especially in a virtual learning context.

This project sheds light on key aspects of a bilingual child's reading process, journal writing practice, multimodal reading responses to culturally relevant literature books, translanguaging in her literacy development, and emergent trilingual development. The findings illustrate how CoCo's bilingual and trilingual literacy practices play a central role in shaping her multilingual and multicultural identity. Furthermore, they highlight the crucial role of family and community in nurturing bilingual and multilingual development and reinforce the perspective that bilingual or multilingual acquisition is an asset, not a deficit, to a child's overall literacy development. By expanding the existing understanding of bilingual and family literacy, this ethnographic case study offers valuable implications for researchers, educators, parents, and community members invested in supporting bilingual and multilingual children.

2

DEVELOPING BILINGUAL LITERACIES

Reading in English and in Mandarin Chinese

Yang Wang & Julie Stensland

This chapter examines CoCo's reading development in two languages, English and Mandarin Chinese, over four years from kindergarten through third grade (from 4:11 to 8:8 indicating from four years and 11 months old to eight years and eight months old). Grounded in the sociopsycholinguistic process of reading (Goodman, 2014), the findings demonstrate a simultaneous emergent bilingual literacy development. The rich description interrogates language learning and literacy development in different dimensions of cognition, linguistics, and sociocultural contexts.

Readers use all the language cueing systems to make meaning, no matter what languages they speak (Goodman et al., 2005). They construct their meaning of the text by using the words on the page in transaction with their own background, purposes, and interests. Meaning-emphasis as an approach to literacy education is a natural development of literacy competency through immersion in real literature and daily writing, resulting in stronger motivation to read and better comprehension after reading (Pressley et al., 2023). When reading a text, children leverage linguistic cueing systems—graphophonics, syntax, and semantics, as well as pragmatic systems—context, prior knowledge, and culture (see Chapter 1), which help them predict upcoming words and construct meaning (Moore & Gilles, 2005). Effective readers engage in purposeful transactions with the texts (Paugh & MacPhee, 2023; Rosenblatt, 2018).

Bilinguals and multilinguals possess a singular linguistic repertoire, similar to monolinguals (García, 2020). Bilingual learners draw upon all their linguistic repertoires when learning the language as well as the content knowledge (García & Li, 2014). Bilingual literacies involve the interlacing of two languages, mixing skills development, meaning construction, and experiences (Musanti &

DOI: 10.4324/9781003517061-2

Rodríguez, 2017) as well as bilingual learners' funds of knowledge (González et al., 2005; Moll, 2014). Bilingual literacies also enable learners to develop concepts and expertise for thinking, listening, speaking, reading, and writing in two languages, making relevant cultural and linguistic connections with what they read and their own experiences to construct meaning (Rubinstein-Ávila et al., 2015). Previous research has identified cross-linguistic relationships, such as phonological awareness, vocabulary development, and reading comprehension between English and Mandarin Chinese, which can support children's bilingual development (Hipfner-Boucher et al., 2014; Lam et al., 2015; Yang et al., 2021).

Language Exposure

CoCo learned to read and write in Mandarin Chinese with me at home. We adopted the textbooks that are commonly used in Mainland China. However, I did not systematically teach pinyin, the phonetic system that was included in the first-grade textbook, for multiple reasons. My major concern was that CoCo might confuse them with English letters (see Chapter 1 for an introduction to the Chinese language). Additionally, my teaching experience informed me that many emergent Chinese readers often rely on pinyin to decode words, which hinders their ability to read texts without pinyin. Instead, I taught CoCo to write Chinese characters, decode characters using their structures and meanings, and understand the texts' meanings. Figure 2.1 shows CoCo taking notes as I explained the new Chinese characters to her. In this photo, I also played a free-access teaching video that I found online as our supplementary teaching material. Beyond learning the content in textbooks, I read many Chinese literature books to her and engaged in discussions about those texts. She practiced copying Chinese characters, wrote short passages after reading texts, and maintained a journal in Chinese.

CoCo grew up in a rich language environment. She owned a home library with hundreds of English and Chinese literature books. I maintained home and office libraries with professional resources and literature books in both languages. We frequently borrowed and read books from each other's collections. We had a steady ritual of nightly storytime and read books in the car when commuting or traveling. She also recorded some Chinese read-aloud videos and book reviews in English on her YouTube channel (https://www.youtube.com/@readwithcoco). Before the COVID-19 pandemic, we visited the local public library on a weekly basis and attended many library story hour events. During the pandemic, we participated in virtual library read-aloud and author events. CoCo often brought books to playdates and babysitting sessions.

CoCo having virtual school allowed me to observe and to gain greater insight into her English literacy development in first grade and second grade. Additionally, I learned about her school experiences from the parent-teacher

FIGURE 2.1 CoCo Taking Notes on New Chinese Characters

conferences, school and classroom newsletters, and our random conversations at home. In both in-person and virtual school learning contexts, CoCo participated in teacher-selected read-aloud, daily independent reading time, reading workshops, weekly library time, and weekly reading buddies time when she read to a younger child at school. CoCo borrowed books from the school library and accessed online or digital reading platforms licensed by her school and district.

Method

Data Collection

Observing CoCo's reading at home, I gathered extensive qualitative data. I often recorded her using my smartphone, iPad, video camera, or digital recorders. The dataset includes numerous audio and video recordings of various reading activities at home; for instance, video clips of her self-selected texts and audio files of conversations after reading. I also maintained observation notes in the notes app using my smartphone, tablet, and computer. Additionally, I interviewed CoCo about her views on being bilingual and her perceptions about reading and asked her to create an artifact—a self-portrait as a bilingual learner (Figure 1.2).

The core data for this chapter consisted of full reading sessions of her reading aloud print texts and retellings, and our reading conferences about those texts. I often provided options or encouraged CoCo to select texts that she wanted to read. Occasionally, I selected texts for her, or we read text excerpts from the books that she was reading. Those texts were either just right for her independent reading level or slightly challenging for her to read independently so that I could mark her miscues—her observed responses—and analyze them. See Chapter 1 for a detailed discussion on miscue analysis. The texts included a variety of picture books, early chapter books, chapter books, and anthology books. The genres included fiction, biography, expository, and essay. I recorded a total of 11 English reading sessions and 15 Chinese reading sessions. Each session was around 30 minutes long.

A typical complete reading session included CoCo reading aloud, retelling the passage, and our reading conferences about her reading and comprehension. Those full reading sessions were conducted following the miscue analysis procedure (see Chapter 1). Miscue analysis is a procedure that emphasizes observation and recording the readers' initial response. Miscues are variations from the text or the reader's observed responses (Goodman et al., 2005). Cold texts—the texts that readers have never read before are often used in miscue analysis to assess the reader's comprehending process during reading and comprehension after reading (Goodman et al., 2005). CoCo read aloud those texts independently using hard copies. Meanwhile, I sat by her and took notes about her miscues and other observations on a notepad. After reading, she retold me the texts by herself, and then I asked aided comprehension questions. I also explored her comprehending process further by asking her reasons for making miscues, borrowing questions from retrospective miscue analysis (RMA) (Goodman et al., 2014; Moore & Gilles, 2005) and over-the-shoulder miscue analysis (Davenport, 2002). For example,

- Does the miscue make sense?
- Does the miscue sound or look like language?
- Was the miscue corrected?
- Why do you think you made this miscue?
- Did it change the meaning of the sentence?
- What connections to other texts or life experiences did you make?

Data Analysis

The full reading sessions were conducted following the miscue analysis procedure (Goodman et al., 2005). Each miscue was coded for graphophonic similarity, syntactic acceptability, semantic acceptability, and meaning change using the in-depth procedure (Goodman et al., 2005). See the book *Reading Miscue*

Inventory (Goodman et al., 2005) or *The Essential RMA* (Goodman et al., 2014) for a detailed discussion of miscue analysis. My two research assistants worked on the miscue marking and coding, retelling scores, and session transcribing in English and Chinese, respectively. One research assistant, Julie, was a monolingual English-speaking doctoral candidate with over 25 years of experience in public education at the school and district levels. The other assistant, whose mother tongue was Mandarin, spoke multiple languages. I reviewed all the markings, codes, scores, and transcriptions and discussed the variations with each assistant for inter-coder reliability (O'Connor & Joffe, 2020). As a parent-researcher (Kabuto & Martens, 2014), I provided a unique perspective to observe CoCo's reading development.

Due to the large number of reading sessions, four English reading sessions and four Chinese reading sessions from each semester of the second and third grades were selected for in-depth analysis and quantitative comparison in Table 2.1. Those sessions were selected because they were completed without interruptions, the English and Chinese sessions were conducted in a similar timeframe for comparing language development, and they provided richer information about her reading and comprehension. The data from other sessions contributed to the observation data.

All the qualitative data were open-coded, and the themes emerged from the data (Stake, 1995). The major themes were identified with the guidance of the theoretical frameworks of reader response theory, reading as a sociopsycholinguistic process, and translanguaging (see Chapter 1). Then, I reported the findings using thick descriptions and examples in this chapter (Stake, 1995). In the following sections, I first describe CoCo's reading in English, then her reading in Chinese, and finally her use of translanguaging.

English Reading

When she read in English, CoCo used all her language systems. She relied on the visual representations of text features and picture clues. Additionally, her prior knowledge helped her comprehend the text. However, her occasional overuse of the graphophonic systems negatively impacted her comprehension.

Relying on Visual Information

When she was five years old, CoCo read many picturebooks. She used all visual information to make meaning in both languages, such as graphic systems, text font, section divider, and pictures. For instance, when she read ***My Teacher is a Monster*** (Brown, 2014; the literature cited are italics with bold as the italic texts are used to indicate the words from the books), she read the name *Bobby* (italic text indicating the print text from the book) as "Baby" (text in quotation marks

TABLE 2.1 Miscue Analysis and Retelling Data from Selected Sessions

	English				*Chinese*			
Grade Level	*Second Grade*		*Third Grade*		*Second Grade*		*Third Grade*	
Date	9/28/21	1/28/22	8/4/22	1/24/23	11/24/21	1/29/22	7/28/22	2/2/23
Text	***Where the Mountain Meets the Moon*** (pp. 4–8)	***Bailey***	***The One and Only Ivan*** (pp.20–33)	***Armed But Not Dangerous***	当世界年纪还小的时候 ***When the World Was Young***	羿射九日 ***Houyi Shoots Down Nine Suns***	父亲树林和鸟 ***Father, Woods, and Birds***	陶罐和铁罐 ***Clay Pot and Iron Pot***
Genre	Fiction	Fiction	Verse novel	Expository	Fairy tale	Folklore	Memoir	Fable
Text length	673	498	1448	493	397	509	465	587
Miscue per hundred words	6	4	4	4	8	9	9	6
Retelling %	80	80	75	82	90	90	75	70
Meaning construction % (no + partial loss)	50	100	66	69	78	70	58	42
Grammatical relation % (strength + partial strength)	81	83	82	79	69	85	78	76
Graphic similarity % (high + some)	93	88	86	91	30	61	29	43
Sound similarity % (high + some)	87	94	88	91	40	56	54	40

indicating the reader's miscue). CoCo explained that the text font was small, and the main character was illustrated small. Hence, she made the miscue due to her prediction from the text feature and the picture.

CoCo mimicked her ELA teacher's way of reading aloud the texts. She read both the print text and the pictorial text to understand the books. Although many of her miscues did not look similar to the text, they did not affect the text's meaning. For example, when reading *I'm playing in my school shoes* in ***Pete the Cat: I Love My White Shoes*** (Litwin, 2010), CoCo read "red shoes" instead because the text *school* was printed in red color. In ***The Dot*** (Reynolds, 2003), she read "carefully" instead of *closely* in *Her teacher picked up the paper and studied it closely* at 5:7 (indicating five years and seven months old).

When CoCo read books with fewer illustrations later in her second and third grades, her miscues showed high graphic and phonic similarities (see data in Table 2.1). It reflects that she relied on the graphophonic systems and valued surface accuracy. However, relying on those did not significantly help her comprehension of the texts.

Using Prior Knowledge

CoCo made inferences from her prior knowledge and the text contexts. For instance, she replaced *watercolors* with "paint" because she had never used watercolors and only had used paint at the time of reading ***The Dot***. Additionally, when she read ***Pete the Cat and the Cool Caterpillar*** (Dean & Dean, 2018), I asked questions to check her comprehension (5:2).

Yang: Where did it go? Did it run away?
CoCo: No, it's right here. <Pointing at the pupa on the next page.>
Yang: How did you know?
CoCo: I just know.
Yang: Where did you learn it?
CoCo: I just know it.
Yang: Did you learn it from school?
CoCo: No.
Yang: Then where did you learn it?
CoCo: 就是那个孙悟空。那里面的书，(毛毛虫) 就变成 this and butterfly. [It is about the Monkey King. In that book, (the caterpillar) became this and butterfly.]

CoCo referred to her prior knowledge which she learned from reading a Chinese book. This knowledge helped her predict and understand this English book.

Another example of CoCo utilizing her prior knowledge is when we talked about the cover of ***Pete the Cat's Train Trip*** (Dean & Dean, 2015). CoCo pointed at the train and said, "高铁 high-speed train" (5:3). By that time, she had never seen a tourist train nor taken one in the United States. However, she took the high-speed train in China a couple of times when visiting our extended family.

Critical Incident: After CoCo Learned the Magic Strategy

In kindergarten and first grade, CoCo effectively used picture clues to make predictions. Her miscues may have looked or sounded different from the texts but often carried similar meanings. For example, she sometimes created nonwords as placeholders while she constructed the meaning from the context. At the end of first grade, she reported many reading strategies, for example, "Look at the pictures, break the words apart, skip the word and come back to the beginning of the sentence, shut the word, look at the words again." Her mimicking of "teacher talk" showed that she started to emphasize using a new strategy. When she read ***Peppa's Chinese New Year*** (EOne, 2018), CoCo turned the book and faced it to me and the camera (5:3).

CoCo: 这是什么 word? [What word is it?]
Yang: George.
CoCo: *George are to.* 你 read 吧，我让你 read. 另外 try to figure out the hard word. 我帮你一起 sight word <pointing at *playgroup*>. 就是 spell it out. 就是 ya-, g-, r-. 我知道这是什么 word 在这里边，所以不要看这两个 word. 这是什么 word？这。这是什么 word? <Blocking the word and only showing ro-.> [You read. I ask you to read. Also, try to figure out the hard word. I can help you do the sight word. That is, spell it out. That is ya-, g-, r-. I know what this word is here, so do not look at those two words. What is this word? This. What is this word?]
Yang: R-O?
CoCo: No. 我在说什么 word？[What word am I saying?]
Yang: Ro? Group.
CoCo: Rou.
Yang: Group, playgroup.

CoCo demonstrated using sounding out for decoding a new word; she started relying on this strategy in her reading after she learned it. She still applied other strategies; however, her top reading strategy shifted, and her reading miscues reflected this change.

CoCo's language learning from school impacted her priority of language system use. When she encountered the new word *ceiling*, she tried to sound it out,

"C is k sound" (6:1). In her piano lesson, CoCo read *a French composer and pianist* as "a French computer and paintist" (6:5). Her miscues of "computer" and "paintist" and the print texts of "composer" and "pianist" looked alike; however, they changed the meaning significantly. When I was reading a professional literacy book for teaching, CoCo looked over and pointed at where I highlighted *Piaget* and asked, "Look. Who is that piglet?" (6:5). CoCo's prioritization of sounds and symbols while ignoring context and not monitoring for meaning resulted in miscues with completely different meanings. Later, she realized that this sounding out strategy may not be effective, "I like to do this strategy. But sometimes it doesn't work. But I am going to try it anyway" (6:8). Even though CoCo was aware that phonics may not help all the time, she chose to use it for efficiency.

When reading a biography of ***Audrey Hepburn*** (Vegara, 2017; 6:5), CoCo read "through" for *though* three times in a row. Those two words look alike; however, they differ in their meanings in the text. Unfortunately, she did not monitor or correct any of them.

> *was scow of real* *through*
> She had a simple rule for life: "Dance as though no
> *through (repeated miscue)*
> one is watching. Sing as though no one can hear
> *through (repeated miscue)*
> you. Live as though heaven is on Earth."

As she continued reading the same text, CoCo read "machine" for *medicine* in the sentence *She helped raise money to provide children with water, food, and medicine*. She shared in our retrospective conversation that she first predicted this word from her own life experience of using a washing machine. Then, she used the context to rethink and learn that it was *medicine*.

Reading ***Coco: My Delicious Life*** (May, 2013) in the ***Lotus Lane*** series, CoCo replaced *Fashion* with "Fraction" in an image (p. 5, 6:8).

Yang: What is (a) fraction?

CoCo: Fraction. I know it. I can tell you. If I use this red notebook and then you want it to divide it into twos for each of us, just cut it equal(ly) into half, and that's called (a) fraction.

Yang: Okay. I love it. Because that could be related to multiplication, right? It's in one area all about math.

CoCo: Yeah.

Yang: However, look at this picture. How does the picture show it's a fraction?

CoCo: En. I think I know. I think the fraction is that these are divided.

Yang: The clothes (in the picture)?

CoCo: I guess this is a fraction. This is a fraction?
Yang: Let's hold on to it and see if we can figure it out.
<We kept on reading.>
Yang: Fraction star? What is it?
CoCo: "Fashion star."
Yang: "Fashion star." What is a fashion star?
CoCo: I think fashion star means … I can, you can break it apart. But sometimes it doesn't. I am gonna turn it anyway. You know a fashion, right? A fashion is someone that knows a lot of dancing …

It could be that CoCo relied on the graphophonic system when reading aloud "fraction" for *fashion*. It could also be that the text and image about *multiplication tables* caused her prediction of "fraction." No matter which way or a mix of both causes, she apparently could connect to her prior knowledge, explaining a fraction. Then, she used the context and image for correction.

When CoCo started second grade, she demonstrated the sound-out strategy and reported using three strategies in her teacher talk—when she pretended to talk like a teacher. Below is how she explained sounding out *Bobby* when she read ***My Teacher is a Monster*** (Brown, 2014),

> You say Bob. You, you take this off b-y. You cover that. Then you take b-o. B is what? B is Bob, right? And then when you get another b, it's bo-bb <holding a longer o sound>. And then what's the y sound? Yuh, yuh. And when you take it together, Bob-be Bobby!

She then shared,

> I just wanted to tell everyone that you can use pictures, words, or sound it out. Those three ones that you can (use). You can just figure out the word. Or you can take what you know and look at the picture, look at the word, and sound it out to do it.

It shows that CoCo valued word decoding and relied on graphophonic systems and visual aids for reading.

Impact of the Magic Strategy

When CoCo started reading texts with fewer illustrations, her reliance on the graphophonic system did not help her overall comprehension. For example, when she read ***Where the Mountain Meets the Moon*** (Lin, 2019; 6:11), her meaning construction was as low as 50% in Table 2.1. She read *Jade Dragon* *was so offended* as "so offered," *thought resentfully* as "thought respectfully," and *is reunited* as "has returned." Her miscues looked and sounded similar to the text; however, they changed meaning significantly. Accordingly, her pursuit of surface accuracy did not help with meaning-making.

CoCo used context to make meaning "in real time" to predict upcoming events and self-corrected her miscues without prompting. She would attempt a word by providing the first part as an attempt to read, then pause, and then correctly read the word in its entirety, e.g., miscue partials when reading ***Bailey Finds a New Home*** (2015). CoCo used the syntactic cueing system when she read unfamiliar words, building upon the sounds she knew to capture the new word after a few attempts (e.g., ***The One and Only Ivan***). When reading, she correctly identified most beginning and ending sounds in the text and demonstrated increased self-correction as she grew as a reader.

In second and third grades, CoCo transferred reading strategies between two languages and was strongly connected to her prior knowledge and experiences. She relied on the graphophonic system when there were no pictures in the texts. Her two reading sessions from third grade showed that she read accurately; however, she struggled to understand the meaning. So, I asked her what reading was, and she responded, "Reading is you look at the words. You talk them out. You still look at the illustrations" (8:5). She shifted from using context clues, prior knowledge, and prior experience to relying on sound and symbols. Her reading view and reading strategies shifted while she built efficiency in third grade.

Comprehension

During the retelling and answering questions about fictional stories, CoCo revealed how she was thinking about the text. She used inference to retell the story and referred to the text by flipping back to certain parts of the story and illustrations to support her thinking with text evidence (e.g., ***Mercy Watson to the Rescue***). She understood the author and illustrator's purpose, connecting meaning through the support of text and pictures (e.g., ***Armed but Not Dangerous***).

CoCo leaned on her funds of knowledge (Moll, 2014) in her inferences during reading and retelling. During reading, she used syntax and picture cues to explain events as they occurred in the story (e.g., ***Audrey Hepburn***). She also explained how the characters felt and described their actions with a sense of familiarity, as though she had personally felt these experiences before for herself and connected these experiences with the feelings and actions of the characters (e.g., ***Mercy Watson to the Rescue***).

In retelling nonfiction text, CoCo understood that all authors write with a purpose. For example, she described how ***Armed but not Dangerous*** (2017) was a cautionary tale and a lesson could be learned from it. She also considered the author of another nonfiction piece on a more personal note. Her interest in going beyond the text was demonstrated in her wanting to question the author of ***Audrey Hepburn*** (Vegara, 2017) about her career as an author.

> Why did you write this book? And is she a real person? And how do you make the book? And what gives you the idea? … When you are grown up, do you want to be a helping wing, a hand wing or hand?
>
> *(5:12)*

CoCo also asked, "How long did it take to illustrate this book, and did it (author) write it the whole day?" Her inquiry questions demonstrated her engagement and comprehension of the texts.

Chinese Reading

Chinese anthologies and literature books for beginning readers are printed with pinyin above the Chinese language characters. Children often rely on pinyin to read these texts. Therefore, the kindergarten and first-grade texts were not included in Table 2.1. However, the observation notes were used for analysis. Similar to her English reading, CoCo used pictures as a visual aid in kindergarten and first grade. All the first-grade texts came with pinyin, and she sometimes relied on those to read. In second grade, she predicted the text from her understanding, and more than half of her miscues were high-quality—meaning did not change. In third grade, she valued surface accuracy and relied on the graphophonics. Overall, CoCo predicted high-quality miscues, although some miscues had low graphic and sound similarity in Table 2.1. Her comprehension was rich. CoCo also constantly connected to her prior knowledge, used the placeholder strategy to read efficiently, and implemented particular methods to decode Chinese characters.

Predicting High-Quality Miscues

CoCo constantly predicted many high-quality miscues from the pictorial text and text context. Those high-quality miscues made sense, but they did not share graphic or phonetic similarities with the text (see Table 2.1). For instance, CoCo read "趴在地上 [lay on the ground]" for *滚在地上 [roll on the ground]*, "年级 [grade]" for *年龄 [age]*, and "野地 [wild field]" for *稻田 [rice field]*. Her miscues had little sound or graphic similarity to the text. Sometimes, even when CoCo reread the same text, she made identical high-quality miscues, demonstrating that she predicted her own texts and did not rely on surface accuracy.

During rereading and retelling, CoCo resolved some Chinese words or noticed her low-quality miscues. However, when she focused on word-level graphic similarity, she lost meaning. For instance, one of her low-quality miscues was "还有 [also]" for *没有 [no]*.

Connecting to Prior Knowledge

CoCo connected to her prior life experience and prior knowledge that she learned from other books or in another language. For example, she borrowed a friend's Chinese name to decode a new word as they shared similar characters. Additionally, CoCo referred to previously read texts and borrowed her prior knowledge for comprehension. For example, she read "灰雀 [sparrow]" instead of *燕子 [swallow]* when she started reading the text of ***The Swallows*** (Zheng, 2018) because she had previously read about sparrows. Also, she read "火焰山 [Flame Mountain]" for *休眠火山 [dormant volcano]*, borrowing her knowledge from reading the fictional book ***Journey to the West***. CoCo also connected 后羿 [Houyi]—the main character in a folktale, to other versions that she had read previously and questioned which version would be authentic. Last, she connected to the prior scientific knowledge of "(the moon) cycling the earth" that she learned in English at school when she talked about ***When the World Was Young*** (Schubiger, 2017).

In contrast, CoCo struggled to understand the text when she lacked prior knowledge. For example, she misunderstood the cause of a fire in one text because the chimney design in a country house was strange to her. In the story of ***Clay Pot and Iron Pot*** (Huang, 2018), CoCo had limited knowledge about the characteristics of iron, so she misunderstood when the iron vase disappeared underground after a long time. This resulted in low meaning construction and overall lower comprehension scores in Table 2.1. Noticing CoCo's lack of relevant background knowledge about this science topic, I helped her learn the differences between clay and iron during her retelling, and she eventually understood the text after rereading.

Meeting New Things

Even though CoCo's preferred strategy when encountering something new was turning to me for help, she also used metacognition and identified her reading strategies. When she was five, she shared, "我可以 just guess 那个 word. [I can just guess that word]." Additionally, her most frequently used strategy was using a placeholder. For example, CoCo spent no time or effort reading new people or place names in either language. Instead, she used a replacement word or a pronoun. She used the pronoun "this" to replace a new city name.

CoCo used context to predict new words. In the example below, she paused for 30 seconds while reading ***When the World Was Young*** (Schubiger, 2017):

P30seconds 却
它一(直) 无法 ^ 决定， ^ 只好……
[It has been unable to decide, so it has to ……]

Yang: 你停在那做什么？[What did you stop there for?]
CoCo: 想。[Thinking.]
Yang: 想什么？[What were you thinking?]
CoCo: 这是什么字。[What word this is.]
Yang: 你是怎么想出来的？[How did you come up with it?]
CoCo: 我试了好几个办法。[I tried several ways.]
Yang: 都有什么？[What are they?]
CoCo: 第一个我就是想"它一直无法什么定"。没想出来。第二个办法—这个字我怎么见过呢，也没有想起来。然后我最后又读一次，"它— " what makes sense. 没想到。最后我又想，想"它一直—"就想想那时候月亮应该干嘛呢。我就想它应该"决定"。然后我就想它这个字可能是 "决定"。[The first thing I thought was that "it has been unable to what decide." But I never figured it out. The second way—I have seen this word before, and I couldn't think of it. Then I read it one last time, "It—" what makes sense. I couldn't think of it. Finally, I thought again, "It has always been—" and then I thought about what the moon should be doing at that time. I just thought it should be "decide." Then I thought that the word might be "decide."]

CoCo explained that she was trying to figure out a word in her long pause. She reported that her first attempt was decoding those four Chinese characters, but she failed to decode one of them. Then she wondered if she had encountered that word before but could not find it. After that, she thought of "what makes sense." Finally, CoCo used context and thought about what the moon was doing; she predicted that the text was *决定 [decide]*. This example also shows her monitoring the reading and using syntax even though the sentence had no word boundaries between Chinese characters (7:1).

In addition to using the context to predict, skipping new things was another frequently used strategy when CoCo read independently. For example, she omitted one character in the example above. Some of her omissions did not change the meaning, and some did. She resolved some omitted new words while retelling. For instance, she deciphered the word *工厂 [factory]* in her retelling of ***The Swallows*** (Zheng, 2018), "然后去那个工，那个房子那去找，然后它又飞到那个房子，那个大工厂的那个地方。噢，这是工厂啊！<with excitement>

[Then it went to look for that, that house, and then it flew to that house, that big factory. Oh, this is a factory!]" It took until the retelling for CoCo to understand the meaning and place in the final piece of her comprehension puzzle. This moment of joy celebrated her individual endeavor to understand the text.

Comprehension and beyond

CoCo created her own transaction to understand (Rosenblatt, 2018) the Chinese texts, and her comprehension went beyond the texts' meaning. That is to say, she compared the text with other previous texts, wondered about the texts, commented on the figure of speech, and expressed her challenges with the expository texts. For example, after CoCo read ***Houyi Shoots Down Nine Suns*** (2017; 7:3), she commented that the story was fictional because "因为之前我知道没有那么多个太阳啊 [Because I know there are not that many suns]." She questioned the reasons why different existing versions of the story mentioned different numbers of suns, "就为什么有的 story 说有 six suns？有的 story 它说有九个 suns. [Then why does one story say six suns? Another story says there are nine suns.]" Her comparison of various texts and her thoughtful questions made her highly engaged in her reading.

After reading ***The Tree from Last Year*** (Niimi, 2018; 7:6) at the end of second grade, CoCo commented that "(我)读得不好。 [(I) did not read well.]" I followed, "哪不好 [what was not good]?" She said, "我不知道那个词 [I don't know that word]." As our dialogue moved on, CoCo asked questions about the bird in the text. She wondered, "它飞走去哪里了？它是怎么想的呢？[Where did it fly? How did it think?]" and "我要是给它唱歌，那树还会听见吗？[If I sing to it, could the tree hear?]" She even commented that the author used personification in the text. Although CoCo understood the text well and gave a thorough retelling, her failure to decode new words bothered her and influenced her self-efficacy.

Critical Incident: Struggling with Comprehension

In third grade, CoCo started reading more nonfiction texts. When she first read the descriptive text in ***The Swallows*** (Zheng, 2018), she almost cried because she was frustrated with retelling. This time, she did not comment on word decoding but explained that she did not understand the meaning.

Yang: 刚才的这个《燕子》都讲了什么？[What is ***The Swallows*** that you just read about?]

CoCo: 不知道，呵呵！[I don't know. Hehe.]

Yang: 你就用你自己的话说一说。[You can use your own words to tell about it.]

CoCo: 我不知道！[I don't know!]
Yang: 怎么会不知道？你刚才不是读下来了吗？[How come you don't know? Didn't you just finish reading it?]
CoCo: 我没理解！[I didn't understand!]
Yang: 你怎么知道你没理解呢？[How do you know you didn't understand it?]
CoCo: 我不知道什么意思！[I don't know its meaning!]

Then, CoCo specifically mentioned that she did not know what the swallows were doing. She retold that they were playing on poles and mentioned that their tails were like scissors, as well as some other details with my probing questions. When asked to specify her reading difficulties, CoCo replied, "The story was hard to understand." Apparently, she was unfamiliar with the genre of expository text, which did not depict a plot in the "story." I tried to help her visualize the scene of the swallows flying by.

Yang: 你现在闭上眼睛，你看看你能不能闭上眼睛想到或是看到这个画面，燕子在飞的画面。[Close your eyes now and see if you can close your eyes and think or see this picture, the picture of swallows flying.]
CoCo: No.
Yang: 为什么？[Why?]
CoCo: My brain, my brain blocks me from thinking.

At that time, she verbalized her struggles and was not confident to share. Additionally, multiple attempts at a new word were frustrating. The first time she met *由 [from]*, she paused for 16 seconds and skipped it; the second time, she paused for 15 seconds and used a replacement with the same meaning; the third time, she read it correctly. After reading, she shared, "那我一开始其实知道，但是我害怕我不对 [I knew (it) in the beginning (when I met it for the first time); however, I was afraid that I was incorrect]." Like her reading in English, she turned to value more accuracy in third grade, and decoding words impacted her reading confidence. I highlighted the strategies that she used (e.g., connecting to a previous text, asking questions, using context clues), praised her for doing the right thing, and encouraged her to be more confident as a reader.

Another reason for CoCo's reticence could be my note-taking while she was reading. She said, "但是我看你弄三篇 notes 了……那你总是写 a lot. [But I saw you took three pages of notes…You always wrote a lot.]" CoCo was concerned about what I wrote in my notes. Therefore, I shared them with her and pointed out that most of those were smart miscues that did not change the meaning. That helped her build her reading metacognition and confidence back again.

Decoding Chinese Characters

Graphic Similarity

CoCo relied on graphic information when she read Chinese texts. A few miscues shared similar meanings with the printed texts. For instance, "凉 [cool]" for *冷 [cold]* and "听道 [hear]" for *知道 [know]*. Those two miscues did not change the text's meaning, and she did not correct them. While many miscues affected her meaning-making, for example, she read "完了[over]" for *院子 [yard]*; "卖 [sell]" or "买 [buy]" for *实 [reality]*, "己 [self]" for *已 [already]*, "体 [body]" for *休 [rest]*, and "比 [compare]" for *此 [this]*. Those Chinese characters look alike; however, adding or missing one stroke makes different characters. In my experience, Chinese-speaking children commonly misuse those words.

Chapter 1 introduces the Chinese language. Phono-semantic compounds are a big category of Chinese characters. Each character carries a meaning component and a sound component. This feature could aid decoding or result in misunderstanding. CoCo used the part to guess the sound of the whole character. For example, "南南" for 喃喃, which ensembles a sound that shares the same pronunciation and does not affect her understanding. However, using one part of a character to sound out affected the meaning in many cases, such as "见在 [see]" for *现在 [now]*, "那里 [that]" for *哪里 [where]*, and "刀 [knife]" for *剪 [scissors]*.

CoCo sometimes used the whole character to sound out an embedded part, while most Chinese-speaking readers used the embedded part to sound out the whole, in my experience. When CoCo first encountered the new word *由 [from]*, she thought it looked like a phono-semantic compound "油 [oil]," and those two characters happened to share the same part. Other examples are "抱住 [hold]" for *包裹 [wrap]*, "翅毛 [wing]" for *羽毛 [feather]*, and "写 [write]" for *与 [and]*. Additionally, CoCo explained her method of decoding the first character in *街坊 [neighbor]*.

> 这个和这个当作这个小 road。因为它们都，因为一 等一下。就是这个它就是，就是这两个偏旁部首，我就把它用成了一个 road，因为这个它有一个横两个横，代表一个 sidewalk。然后这个就是这两个也有，可以把它弄平，也是两个 sidewalk。两个 sidewalk连在一起就是街，然后上面这里面是个小人，两个人走。
>
> [Take this and this as this little road. Because they all, because—Wait a minute. This is it, it is these two radicals, I used it as a road, because it has a horizontal and two horizontals, representing a sidewalk. Then there are these

two, which can be flattened, and they are two sidewalks. The two sidewalks are connected together to form a street, then there is a villain on the top, and two people walk.]

Although *街 [road]* is a phono-semantic compound, she identified it as an ideogrammic compound with two pictographic parts. CoCo created her own way of recognizing words from their visuals.

Sound Similarity

Some challenging words in the text were printed with pinyin—the sound system above those words. Although CoCo prioritized using the character graphics, she used pinyin to read aloud. She relied on pinyin graphics and sounds. For instance, "gēn" for *gēng*, "dǎn" for *diǎn*, "cén" for *céng*, and "què" for *qiè*. CoCo misused the pinyin sound of *eng* with the English sound */en/* because English doesn't share the same *eng*, *ian* and *q* sounds from Chinese pinyin. Additionally, she mixed the second (rising) tone and the fourth (down) tone, such as "lì" for *lí*, and "nìng" for *níng*. Sound and tone changes in Chinese can result in completely different words.

Many Chinese characters are polyphones, sharing different sounds. The variation of sound marks different meanings. Readers need to identify the sound from the context. For example, 长 cháng 腿的萝卜 [long legs turnip] versus 长 zhǎng 腿的萝卜 [the turnip growing legs]. When CoCo read the picturebook *长腿的萝卜* ***The Turnip with Legs*** (2009), she should have read the latter instead of the former according to the meaning of the story. In another context, CoCo misread the same word for the same reason.

The Chinese language has many homophones—characters that share the same sound but look different. CoCo often used a homophone that she knew to mark the sound of new words when she read independently. For instance, she used "天 [sky]" to mark the sound of *添 [add]* and "无 [no]" for *梧 [maple]*. The reason could be that CoCo learned characters before learning pinyin, and it was efficient for her to mark with homophones instead of using pinyin, which she often confused with English phonetics.

Translanguaging

CoCo used her linguistic repertoire (Canagarajah, 2011; García & Li, 2014) when she read. She borrowed English phonetics to sound out Chinese pinyin, created her hidden connectors between two languages to help her decode word sounds and word meaning, and transferred to the other language to make meaning and express her important messages. Her translanguaging when she read and talked about the English texts was not as active as her reading in Chinese.

Borrowing English Sound

CoCo read pinyin and spoke Chinese without any phonetic accent. However, she could not write pinyin proficiently for given Chinese words. I did not teach her pinyin because I was concerned that she would rely on pinyin to decode the sounds of words and that she might confuse them with English letters and phonetics. Therefore, when she read independently, CoCo borrowed English phonetics to sound out Chinese words. For instance, she used the English letter "N" to help her learn the Chinese character 恩 ēn [kindness], which shares the same sound.

When she marked the sound for unknown words, CoCo attempted to use pinyin. However, she often ended up borrowing English phonetics without realizing the differences. For instance, she used English *o* for Chinese compound vowels *ou* and *ao*. She marked "chō" for 收 *shōu [receive]*, and "zò" for 造 *zào [make]*. She used English *a* sound for Chinese compound vowels *ui* or *ei*, for example, "gwā" for 规 *guī [regulation]*, and "wā" for 威 *weī [power]*. Some sounds are unique combinations with one vowel and one special consonant or double vowels like *ian* and *uo*. She marked "bàn" for 遍 *biàn [time]* and "gwǒ" for 裹 *guǒ [wrap]*.

CoCo borrowed the English sound of "j" when reading aloud 锯 jù [saw]. However, it sounded like zhù in Chinese. When she marked the sound by herself in the third grade, she marked 锯 as "zhú" instead of jù. English doesn't have the *j* and *ü* sounds. Also, she misused the second rising tone *ú* for the fourth falling tone *ù*. It showed that she mixed the rising tone with the Spanish accent. These markers looked the same above the vowels in both languages; however, they indicated the vowel was stressed in Spanish and had a rising tone in Chinese. This confusion also showed when she learned Spanish in Chapter 5.

Hidden Connectors

CoCo created hidden connectors from a mesh of two languages that can only be identified by bilingual speakers. She created a medium to connect sound, visuals, and meaning by using homophones, words with multiple meanings, and compound words (see Table 2.2).

The first type was homophone connectors between CoCo's English notes and the new Chinese characters in Table 2.2. When she met 愉快 (its pinyin is marked as yú kuài and its meaning is happy) for the first time, CoCo asked for the pronunciation of the first character 愉. After hearing yú, she marked "fish" by this character. However, fish was not its meaning, nor was it close to the pronunciation. Her hidden connector was the Chinese homophone for fish 鱼, which sounded the same as 愉, even though they were not related in terms of graphic similarity or meaning. This hidden connector seemed to be an extra step

TABLE 2.2 Hidden Connectors

Expected Response	*Hidden Connector*	*Observed Response*
New Chinese Character (same sound/Chinese pinyin)	***Homophones***	*English Marker (same meaning)*
yú kuài 愉快 [happy]	yú 鱼	fish
xiāng xià 乡下 [countryside]	xiāng 香	sweet
One Translation	***Multiple Meanings***	*Alternate Translation*
奶奶 [from the dad's side]	grandmother	姥姥 [from the mom's side]
全国 [nationwide]	entire country	整国 [whole country]
One Part	***Compound Words***	*The Other Part*
常常 [often]	非常 [very]	非非 [nonword]
齐 [together]	思齐 [a friend's name]	思 [think]

to learning the new word. However, it was an efficient way for CoCo to mark and remember.

The second type of hidden connector was words with multiple meanings in Table 2.2. CoCo knew the text's meaning in English; however, the same English word can be translated into two equivalent Chinese words. Her miscues and the printed text may have looked different, but they shared the same English translation. For example, *奶奶* and *姥姥* are both translated into grandmothers.

CoCo borrowed parts of some compound words to help her decode words. This was the third type of hidden connector that she used in Chinese only. She misused the two characters in an AB structure word. She was supposed to borrow B, but she borrowed A or vice versa. For example, she meant to borrow 常 from 非常 to read *常常* but she read it as "非非." She meant to borrow *齐* from 思齐 but ended up reading "思."

Embedding English Syntax in Chinese

CoCo mixed the grammar rules between the two languages. For example, she embedded English sentence structure in her use of Chinese, "读他一本书 [Read him a book]." The common way to address it is *给他读一本书 [For him read a book].* Another example is "它闪亮是一个很好的东西 [It shining is a very good thing]." The usual sentence structure order should be *它能闪亮很好 [It can shine very good].* When Chinese syntax influenced her English reading, it was marked as a syntactical dialect. For example, she sometimes left out -ed endings for past tense. The Chinese language uses a past tense marker instead of changing the word format (Wang & Yang, 2007; see more in Chapter 1).

Translating for Meaning

CoCo borrowed English words to predict unknown Chinese words and expressions and communicate efficiently. Sometimes, CoCo knew the meaning of a Chinese word but did not know the pronunciation. She then gave the English equivalent. For instance, she read "该桃" for *核桃 walnut*. Her miscue showed a nonsense word with high graphic similarity. She explained its meaning in English but did not know how to pronounce the first Chinese character. Moreover, when CoCo encountered new Chinese words, she often used English words to help her understand the new words' meanings and marked English meanings by the texts. For example, she marked "box" by *盒*, "hide" by *藏着*, and "fishing" by *钓鱼*.

CoCo used English to explain the word's meaning when we talked about the texts. When I said "潮湿," she gave the meaning, "moist." When we discussed ***Father, Woods, and Birds*** (Niu, 2018) about birds in the woods during daybreak, she misunderstood *黎明 límíng dawn* for a homophone *鹂鸣 bird chirping* and explained, "(it means) sound, sound as a signal." After I pointed out they were homophones, she explained *dawn* in the text "是春天的早上 [is spring morning]. Sun is already up." CoCo used English for explanations. She also translated into English for reassurance and confirmation. When she discussed *beak*, she first said the word in Chinese and added its English translation. Besides, CoCo mixed English and Chinese to explain word meanings and discuss the text efficiently. For example, when she explained *年迈*, she said, "就是非常 old [(it) is very old]." In one retelling, she asked, "我可以说 [Can I say] whatever I want to?" She mixed two languages together for efficiency.

Transferring for Meaning

CoCo's translanguaging shows her comprehension and the purpose and function of language use. She transferred more actively when reading Chinese. CoCo talked in English to preview a page of a Chinese story and to mark the closure of a retelling, "The end" and "That's it." Once, she said the English words "comma" and "period" to mark her punctuation in Chinese oral retelling. CoCo even borrowed English for transitions, "at the beginning of the story" and "That's the meaning of ..." She used the English word "lesson" in the retelling, "这里边的 lesson 它就说...[The lesson here is ...]."

Moreover, CoCo borrowed English to highlight the themes of the Chinese texts. After reading ***The Tree From Last Year*** (Niimi, 2018) about a bird's revisit to a tree, she shared that the text was about "鸟和树的 friendship [the bird and the tree's friendship]" and "friends are friends forever." Additionally, CoCo switched to English for her comments like "(it) doesn't sound real" and to highlight the author's point and compare "story" and "real life" after reading ***Clay Pot and Iron Pot***. For example, she explained, "有可能 the author made it like 这个铁罐给摔碎了。...但是在 real life 的时候我就觉得不能摔碎。[It's possible that the author made it like the iron pot was broken.... But in real life, I feel that it cannot be broken.]" Last, CoCo also used English to share her feelings. For example, she struggled to read ***The Swallows*** (Zheng, 2018) and said, "My brain blocks me from thinking." When asked why the author wrote the text, she commented in English, "I don't know," and then said, "to confuse us."

When reading in English, CoCo used Chinese as the functional language to facilitate her speaking. For example, "所以我们继续。我让你看一个 page. [So, let's continue. Let me show you a page.]" Before reading, she sometimes chose Chinese language to share her prior knowledge. During reading, she used Chinese to describe the text structure, explain her interpretation, and make inferences. She also borrowed Chinese to confirm her understanding and show her confusion by responding "明白。[I understand.]" "是对的。[That's right.]" "这道题我不知道。[I don't know this question.]" Her translanguaging during her reading, retelling, and discussion contributed to her comprehending and comprehension of the texts (Goodman et al., 2005).

Discussion

CoCo's strategies in English shifted as she learned and progressed from kindergarten to third grade. In kindergarten, she used visual support from the illustrations in picturebooks for making predictions and comprehending. As she learned phonics in kindergarten and first grade, she began sounding out words and consciously identified this strategy in her reading, although she employed a range of dynamic reading strategies, including applying prior knowledge, context clues, visual aids from the images, and others. When she read early chapter books with less illustration support, she increasingly relied on the graphophonic systems for decoding. By second grade, on one hand, CoCo still applied those dynamic reading strategies mentioned above and made high-quality miscues that did not change the meaning of the text. On the other hand, she relied on the graphophonic system, which made an impact later in third grade. In particular, she pursued surface accuracy in third grade and had more low-quality miscues that shared high graphic similarity but changed the meaning of the texts. CoCo still used various strategies of applying prior knowledge and predicting from the contexts; however, she placed more value on graphic similarity and surface accuracy, which hindered her reading confidence and comprehension. Observations of CoCo's reading showed that sole reliance on graphophonics, that is to say, prioritizing decoding words only and focusing on surface accuracy, did not support her comprehension. As a result, it disrupted her confidence and interfered with her identity as a bilingual reader. I hope it was just a temporary phase in her bilingual development. Moving forward, it will be important to reinforce her use of other effective and efficient strategies as reading should be a continuous transaction among the reader, text, and context to make meaning (Rosenblatt, 1978/1994). Bilingual readers, in particular, benefit from drawing upon all systems of languages, their schema, and funds of knowledge to construct meaning (Goodman et al., 2005; Moll, 2014).

Since first grade, CoCo's dominant instructional language has been English. The strategies that she learned from language instruction at school not only shaped her English literacy but also influenced her home language learning and reading. Over time, CoCo started to value accuracy and became more self-conscious about making miscues in her reading. In third grade, she encountered a broader range of genres and nonfiction texts on various topics. She recognized that understanding the meaning was the key, and lacking prior knowledge made comprehending difficult. Building her prior knowledge before reading became necessary. CoCo initiated her funds of knowledge (Moll, 2014), no matter which languages she accessed. As an educator, I could support her by encouraging discussions about her reading, emphasizing meaning-making, ensuring diverse language input, and validating her use of funds of knowledge. However, many children from other families may not receive such support at home, highlighting the crucial role of school instruction in shaping children's bilingual literacy development.

With the unique characteristics of the logographic Chinese language, CoCo could better predict the text's meaning. However, this overreliance on visual cues sometimes resulted in low-quality miscues with high graphic similarity but differed in meaning. When reading Chinese texts as an emergent reader, CoCo simultaneously applied two systems of visual symbols—Chinese characters and pinyin, which made the process more complicated. Because she learned the characters first, she relied primarily on the character visuals rather than pinyin for decoding. Additionally, she used the semantics system as many Chinese characters carry intrinsic meaning. However, the prevalence of homophones and polyphones in the Chinese language required her to use context and prior knowledge for accurate interpretation. This underscores the importance of contextual understanding in both English and Chinese reading.

Bilingual reader identity is not divided between those two languages but is built on the full linguistic repertoire (García & Li, 2014). CoCo utilized both English and Chinese to comprehend texts, regardless of which language she was reading. Her reading strategies transferred between two languages for the purpose of efficient and effective meaning-making. Translanguaging is a unique way for bilingual children to comprehend text in either language efficiently (García & Li, 2014). Furthermore, cultural and linguistic connections played a crucial role in her reading experience. CoCo developed her own hidden connectors–homophones, words with multiple translations, and combined words—to facilitate decoding and understanding. Different bilingual learners may have varied ways of creating their hidden connectors due to differences between languages, reading strategy uses, and personal preferences. Although those connectors vary on the surface, they help readers transact (Rosenblatt, 2018). Recognizing and validating these hidden connectors can empower bilingual readers to embrace literacy in both languages. It shows that bilingual readers engage in the interlacing of two languages, mixing skill development, meaning construction, and experiences (Musanti & Rodríguez, 2017).

Translation plays an important role in bilingual communication in real life (Baker, 2014), and CoCo was accustomed to translating and transferring while reading. Whether translating a single word, a full sentence, or an entire passage, her ability to do so demonstrated both her comprehension and bilingual proficiency. Translating longer discourses reflected advanced word decoding, syntactic knowledge, and familiarity with common expressions. It also indicated deep comprehension in one language and strong proficiency in both languages.

The unpacking of comprehension, retelling, and talking about her miscues that occurred post-reading helped CoCo refine her understanding of the text, clarify misconceptions, and gain deeper meaning from the text. This chapter expanded the previous research of RMA with monolingual children and young English language speakers (Hao & Wang, 2022; Moore & Gilles, 2005; Wang & Seale, 2019). Regardless of the language, engaging in meaningful conversations like RMA helped the bilingual child, CoCo, build the strategy toolkit to become an independent reader, increase her confidence and agency, and strengthen her bilingual reader identity.

Implications

These findings contribute to a deeper understanding of bilingual literacy development and offer valuable educational implications for bilingual teachers, as well as educators who work with students using non-alphabetical languages. Bilingual researchers can extend this work by examining how bilingual readers engage with texts in other language pairs. Longitudinal studies following bilingual students across multiple contexts, such as school, family, and community, would provide further insights into the complexities of bilingual language use.

A thorough understanding of the bilingual reading process can help educators and teachers bridge the differences between multiple languages and support bilingual students in achieving academic success. Since bilingual learners do not follow a standardized path, a one-size-fits-all approach is ineffective. Instead, bilingual teachers can adopt a kidwatching approach, assessing what children can do independently and with scaffolding. In this sense, the children become teachers—active participants in their own learning. Kidwatching, as described by Goodman and Owocki (2002), provides teachers with an opportunity to evaluate and value children and their learning. Evaluation should come from close observation of their learning process instead of sole reliance on curriculum-based and standardized test scores. Educators can help children build bridges and prior knowledge, and be exposed to a wide range of topics and materials. They must allow opportunities for children to talk about their hidden connectors and value this unique way of meaning-making. This unpacking of comprehension that occurs post-reading can help guide teachers' next steps in questioning and facilitating rich conversations to gain profound meaning and understanding. This conversation is an important instructional guide for the next steps to build the strategy toolkit for independent readers.

Furthermore, educators must support equitable practices by leveraging the cultural and linguistic wealth children bring to their classrooms. The connection between home and school is critical to emergent biliteracy learners. Educators must build this relationship by creating an open dialogue with families about the literacy practices occurring in the home and those demonstrated and used in the classroom. Recognizing the home language and building upon that experience with literacy learning in the classroom provides a connection for young learners. This affirms that the child's culture, language, and family identity are a critical connection for maintaining the home language and the continued development of English as a written and spoken language.

Parents and community partners, such as the public library, cultural associations, and advocacy groups, can provide resources to support a bilingual environment at home. No matter what languages the children use, meaning-making is the purpose of reading. Home reading conferences provide a space for children to explore deep meaning and use their languages. This is particularly important when parents want their children to keep their heritage language. Parents can purposefully use more heritage language in their conversations, which would help children acquire and use those languages.

Inquiry Questions

Questions for Researchers:

- How do bilingual children develop bilingual literacies at school and at home?
- How do children form their bilingual and bicultural identities?

Questions for Teachers:

- How can teachers use translanguaging to develop emergent bilingual children's literacy skills?
- How can teachers challenge monolingual approaches and incorporate multilingual teaching strategies in a diverse classroom?
- How can teachers make education more equitable for multilingual students?

Questions for Parents:

- How can bilingual parents support their children's bilingual reading development?
- How can parents help maintain children's heritage languages and cultures?
- How can first-generation immigrant parents build their children's bilingual identities?

Suggested Reading

Baker, C. (2014). *A parents' and teachers' guide to bilingualism* (4th ed.). Multilingual Matters.

Kabuto, B. (2010). *Becoming biliterate: Identity, ideology, and learning to read and write in two languages*. Routledge.

Kabuto, B. (2022). *Becoming bilingual readers: Identity, translanguaging, and biographic biliteracy profiles*. Routledge.

3

A THOUSAND DAYS OF JOURNALING

A Multilingual, Multimodal, Multigenre Home Writing Practice

In elementary and middle school, my teachers assigned journal writing as the only writing assignment during summer and winter breaks. I wrote about seeing train tracks for the first time, staying up for the Chinese New Year countdown, hiking with friends in a forest park, watching historical dramas and news on television, etc. Later, I also journaled throughout my four years of college. Journaling was first a childhood writing practice, and then it became my personal space for recording my life, expressing my thoughts, and connecting with others. Naturally, when my daughter CoCo began kindergarten, I introduced her to journaling as a way to foster her writing skills and provide a space for her to use her heritage language. Research suggests that children should be encouraged to write in their minority languages as much as they can (Cunningham, 2020), and journaling can serve as a valuable writing practice for their heritage language development.

This chapter presents CoCo's heritage language and literacy development through her journal writing experience. Over the years, she filled ten journal books comprising over 1,000 journal entries from kindergarten to third grade (Figure 3.1), which were all collected as the dataset. Our practice also involved me sitting by CoCo, observing as she wrote, and then listening to her reading aloud her entries. Her sharing helped me gain more insights into her purposes, language use, and emergent writing development.

For analysis, I examined all of CoCo's journal entries and open-coded every piece using descriptive coding (Miles et al., 2020), borrowing the theoretical frameworks of translanguaging and multimodality (see more in Chapter 1). Several categories emerged from the codes, and I read across all the categories for major themes. The four major themes are her development as a writer, language

DOI: 10.4324/9781003517061-3

FIGURE 3.1 CoCo's Ten Journal Books

development and translanguaging use, use of multiple modes, and cultural connections.

Writer Development

CoCo's journal writing process developed through four phases over four years when reflecting on her effort and my scaffolding (Vygotsky, 1978), as delineated below:

Phase I: She narrated, and I wrote (from 5:2, indicating five years and two months old). CoCo told me what she wanted to write down. She talked in English and I translated her English words into Chinese. She sometimes traced the words and marked punctuations in a sentence. Then, we read the journal together.

Phase II: She narrated, I wrote, and she filled in some words (from 5:4). CoCo told me what she wanted to write. When it came to words that I thought she could write by herself or with a little help from me, I passed her the pen and the journal book. After we finished the journal entry, we read it together.

Phase III: She wrote, and I filled in the new words (from 5:10). CoCo wrote down as much as she possibly could, and I gave her the new words. I often suggested better word choices for her. During this phase, I wrote my own journals to demonstrate and encourage her to write independently. (See Figure 3.2, left part.)

Phase IV: She wrote, I gave the new words, and she copied them (from 6:10). CoCo journaled independently and left the new words blank. After she finished writing, she asked for those new words. I wrote them on the side, and she copied them into the blanks that she left. She occasionally read the journal aloud to share. (See Figure 3.2, right part.)

We followed the Chinese journal format, including the date (in the order of month, date, and the day of a week) and weather on the top (see Figure 3.2). In Phases I and II, CoCo drew pictures along with the text, and we used colored pens to write. After she had taken over writing, she used a pencil for easy erasing and correcting. Since the pandemic started, we numbered each journal entry at the top right corner to record the number of days we would be quarantined. Unfortunately, it lasted longer than we all expected. On day 883, CoCo returned to the in-person classroom. We ended up numbering until the end of third grade.

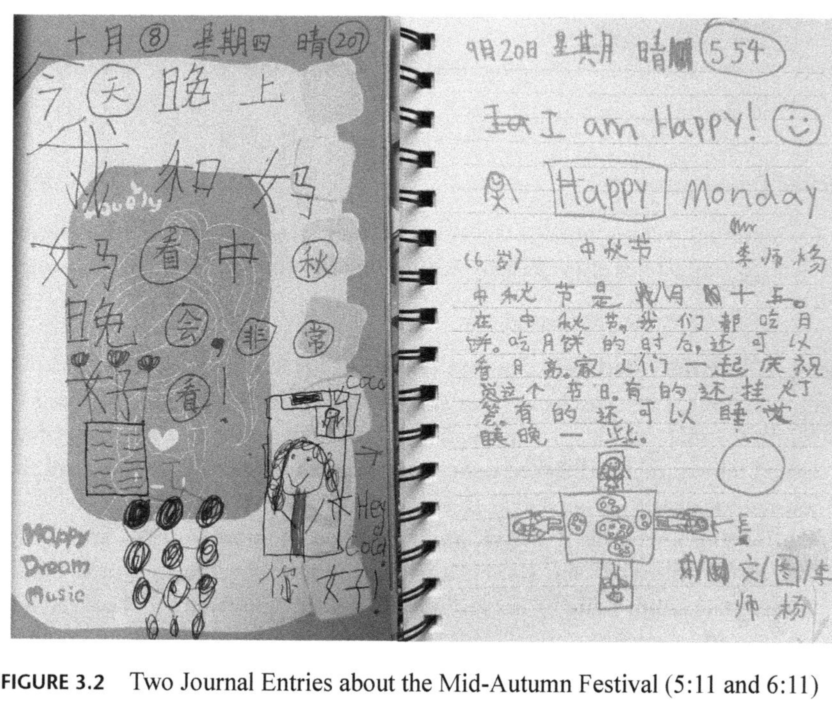

FIGURE 3.2 Two Journal Entries about the Mid-Autumn Festival (5:11 and 6:11)

Journal Topics

CoCo's journal recorded a wide range of topics. When she ran out of ideas, she sought suggestions from me or her dad and often drew inspiration from our conversations. When we traveled, or when a particular subject intrigued her, she wrote about it in two or more consecutive entries. During Phase II, as mentioned above, we included a brief list of daily activities. By Phases III and IV, she either documented her entire day or focused on a specific event. The pandemic influenced many of her entries, reflecting virtual and outdoor activities. After returning to in-person school in third grade, her journal increasingly featured school-related experiences. Her journal topics can be categorized into ten broad themes, and I list a few examples for each category:

- Home-related: crafts, tea parties, birthdays, picnics
- Connection with extended family: online videochat, lǎolao (maternal grandma) learning English, conversations with other relatives
- Family trips: beach outings, camping, road trips
- School-related: virtual learning, talent shows, testing, recess
- Writing & learning: science and social studies topics, Chinese language expressions, favorite books
- Extracurricular activities: music lessons, sports, recitals
- Outdoor activities: hiking, stargazing, a boat ride
- Community events: a kids' marathon, state fairs, farmer's markets
- Cultural events: American and Chinese holidays and events, Chinese cultural entertainment, international festivals
- Personal emotions and care: losing a tooth, doctor appointments, birthday wishes

When the COVID-19 pandemic started in China, CoCo created a banner expressing support for the Chinese people. The pandemic's influence permeated her life and the journal, too. In her journal, CoCo recorded moments like maintaining social distance when her teacher and friends visited. She noted health precautions such as wearing masks, avoiding direct contact with objects, and using tongs to pick up Halloween candies. She also expressed her longing to return to in-person school, designed a poster advocating for it, drew an illustration of a girl wearing a mask, and even created a riddle about the name of a Chinese doctor.

Multiple Genres

CoCo's journal books encompassed a variety of genres, reflecting her creative exploration of different writing styles. While many entries were narratives, she also experimented with thematic writing, focusing on topics such as a person she liked, her favorite animal or space, her superpower, and "All About Me."

CoCo created original fictional stories inspired by the literature that she read and her experiences, including "胡萝卜的小女孩 [the carrot's girl. Brackets indicate English translation and correct spelling]," "Bird in the backyard 后院的鸟," and "李小姐日记 [Miss Li's Diary]." In some instances, she rewrote a storybook or added an alternative ending to another story. After reading a multi-ending text in a Chinese textbook, she crafted multiple conclusions for her own story about a walking piano. She also incorporated moral reflections, marking messages from some of her stories at the end, such as "释义明理" [explanation and moral], and promoting readers with questions like, "WHAT IS THE MAIN IDEA OF THE WHOLE PASSEGE [passage]? (Hint: It is not one word.)" All texts in the quotation marks indicate CoCo's original language use and spelling.

Our shared reading of ancient Chinese poetry also influenced her writing. CoCo memorized many classical poems and composed her poems following those poems with four-line structure, strict word count, and rhyming rules. In addition, she experimented with modern free-verse poetry on topics like summer, love, sunshine, the piano, a little baby, beach, etc. After learning about Haiku from school, she wrote one about flowers.

CoCo also wrote expository texts based on new knowledge that she acquired, covering subjects such as cells, the life cycle, wind, plants, and musical instruments. Her nonfictional writing included bullet points of birthday activities, recommendations for playing piano, steps for writing Chinese characters, and the history of the Great Wall. She sometimes incorporated the Q&A format to show facts and added glossaries. She also designed charts and graphs to compare seasons, food, and people.

Beyond traditional writing, CoCo frequently incorporated interactive elements into her journal. She designed fill-in-the-blank exercises, math questions, piano practice activities, guess-it games, and jokes. She also composed letters to the tooth fairy (see Figure 3.3), notes to me, and thank-you cards. Additionally, CoCo designed comics, song lyrics, and strands of text messages to represent dialogues. CoCo constantly blended multiple genres within a single entry, demonstrating her creativity and flexibility in written expression.

Authorship

CoCo developed her writing conventions and identity as an author through journaling. I introduced her to journal formats, handwriting, complete sentences, and paragraphs, which she gradually acquired. In the beginning, CoCo wrote large Chinese characters randomly across multiple print lines. To help her, I drew boxes and taught her to write within them. She then noticed paragraph

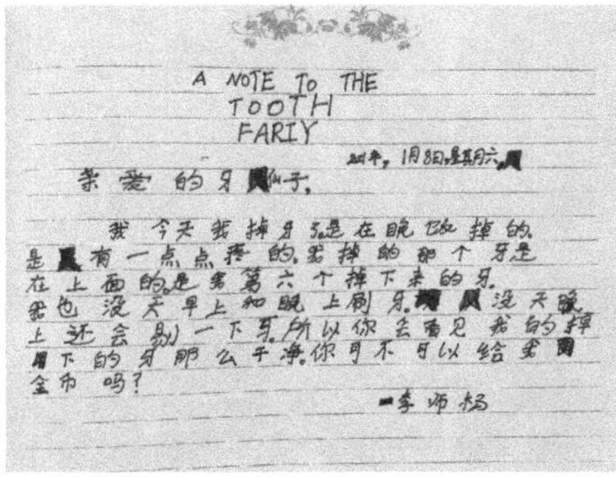

FIGURE 3.3 A Note to the Tooth Fairy (6:2)

structures and began numbering them at the beginning of each paragraph. When she left a margin on the left side instead of indenting the first line of a paragraph, I demonstrated proper indentation by drawing lines for her and explaining formatting rules.

Over time, CoCo added titles to some journal entries. She also embellished with emotional descriptions and emojis by the dates and weather descriptions. For example, in Figure 3.4, CoCo wrote, "I am happy!" followed by a smiley face emoji. She also experimented with capitalization to highlight place names, song titles, people's titles, and emotions, such as "XXX NASHNOLL PARK [XXX National Park], PUT UP THE TENT with dad!!!!!" Moreover, CoCo learned to use punctuation marks as well as quotation marks for dialogues and parentheses for explanations. For instance, she marked homophones, added reasons, introduced her friend "Lewis (my friendly friend)," and expressed her inner voice "都没有哭（我心哭了） [I didn't cry (my heart cried)]." Furthermore, she invented her own abbreviations for some English words, for example, "DD" for "Disney downtown."

CoCo took pride in her journals and saw herself as an author. She marked her authorship on many journal entries, like signing her name as the author and the illustrator, then added her age by the author's place and even included her gender in one entry. She picked up that idea from a Chinese children's magazine that we subscribed to. Inspired by picture books, CoCo also added the author's bio and the author's note. For instance, in one poem about lemons (7:3), CoCo added "Note from Arther [Author]" denoting facts about lemon trees from her as the author. She actively observed those text features and designed hers following those mentor texts.

CoCo's journal style evolved from personal to social and from recording for herself to seeking interactions with her pretend audience. She often imagined her journal book as a close friend; therefore, she included greetings at the beginning

FIGURE 3.4 CoCo Writing Her Journal (6:10)

and farewells at the end. Her writing invited interaction with her other pretend readers in various ways: marking "未完，待续 [to be continued]," sharing the lessons learned in English and the word/quote/lesson of the day in text boxes, asking questions like "Do you think it is sily [silly]? Yes No," grading her own journal by commenting "nice job" and making an evaluation chart in two languages. Her journals also featured endnotes for new words and their meanings, interactive activities such as drawing musical notes with instructions, a series of piano activities, math problems, and text boxes for facts.

In her first-grade and second-grade classes, CoCo shared her journal books during her show-and-tell time. She deeply connected with Anne Frank's story and recorded in one entry (5:7) that she read Anne Frank's Diary (Folman, 2018).

> 今天我和妈妈一起读安妮的一个书。安妮的日记全世界最有名的日记。我觉的（得）安妮的（日）记很好玩。
>
> [Today my mother and I read one book about Anne. Anne's Diary (The Diary of Anne Frank) is the most famous diary in the world. I think Anne's Diary is very interesting.]

CoCo aspired to publish her own journal and share it with a wider audience, showcasing her strong author identity and writing agency. She took ownership of her journal, her story, and her journey, using writing as a means to document her connection to the world.

Language Learning

One of the primary purposes of journaling was for CoCo to practice writing in Chinese. While she mainly wrote in Chinese, she incorporated English for ease of expression or when she lacked the necessary Chinese vocabulary. This practice aligns with the concept of translanguaging, where bilingual and multilingual individuals draw from their linguistic repertoires as a whole (García et al., 2017). When CoCo wrote, she used a large linguistic repertoire—Chinese, English, and some Spanish—instead of relying on one individual language. She used translanguaging efficiently based on her writing needs.

Starting from the first day of virtual school at home, we structured her first journal to support bilingual writing: we listed activities in English on the left page and wrote narratives in Chinese on the right page. This allowed her to engage with both languages in a meaningful way. She consistently wrote dates in both languages, demonstrating an early awareness of bilingual conventions. The first complete English sentence that she wrote was "Today I lnrd [learned] the clock." "It is horatnor [It is hot out here] (5:6)." She started writing more words in the summer as a rising first grader and wrote the first complete Chinese sentence, "早上我出去了。[I went out this morning.] (5:9)" Her first complete journal was "我今天和哥哥姐姐在游泳池里玩。[I played with my brother and sister (close friends) in the pool today.] (5:10)" CoCo started writing independently on Day 139 (5:9). After Day 600 (seven years old), she was learning in an English-dominant environment, increasingly incorporating English vocabulary when describing schoolwork.

To strengthen her Chinese language skills, I intentionally introduced her to new words so she could embed them into her writing. For example, I taught her some transitional words for time sequence. When she reused those transitional words later, she highlighted them within the text and compiled a glossary list of them on her own. Then, she created her practice suggestions for her readers, reinforcing her learning process. I encouraged her to borrow words and phrases from mentor texts, such as Chinese textbooks and literature books, to enrich her writing.

Mixing English and Chinese Codes

When encountering unfamiliar Chinese characters, CoCo employed various strategies, including using Chinese pinyin—the phonetic alphabets, English words, and illustrations. This ability to switch between different symbol systems and incorporate visuals contributed to her writing fluency. CoCo transferred to English words in her journal when she referred to real people's names (e.g., friends, classmates, teachers, authors, or fictional characters from books and media (e.g., Peppa Pig, Fancy Nancy, Superman, Mary Poppins). Similarly, she used English names for place names, including grocery stores, parks, cities, states, countries, and landmarks (e.g., Big Ben, Niagara Falls).

CoCo's writing also reflected her everyday linguistic experiences. She borrowed her play language and school language in English (e.g., monkey bars, treasure box, cartwheel, quiet time, homework pass). She wrote English for words that she had initially acquired in that language (e.g., pizza, applesauce, gingerbread man, picnic, crocs), as well as book and song titles. CoCo often embedded other English nouns within Chinese sentences. As illustrated in Figure 3.5, she combined a mix of codes—pinyin, picture, English, and Chinese for this sentence, "toǔ [tú] toe 了 [painted her toes.]" In a separate journal where she shared her tips for playing piano, she listed English musical terms, provided Chinese explanations for each one, and embellished with small pictures. Occasionally, CoCo used English as a placeholder, writing an English word when she did not know the Chinese equivalent during her writing and then later replacing it upon learning the correct word. For example, she marked a star by the word "cookie **" and later added the Chinese word "饼干."

CoCo used bilingual representation for emphasis. For example, she translated numbers from one language to the other, provided clarifications in the alternate language like "Trunck-or-Treat (要糖)," and recorded both languages such as "red envelope 红包," "American dollars 美元," and "PJ day 睡衣日." Additionally, CoCo translated full sentences into English, such as "我很棒！I'm very amazing!" and even translated an English song she learned at school into Chinese.

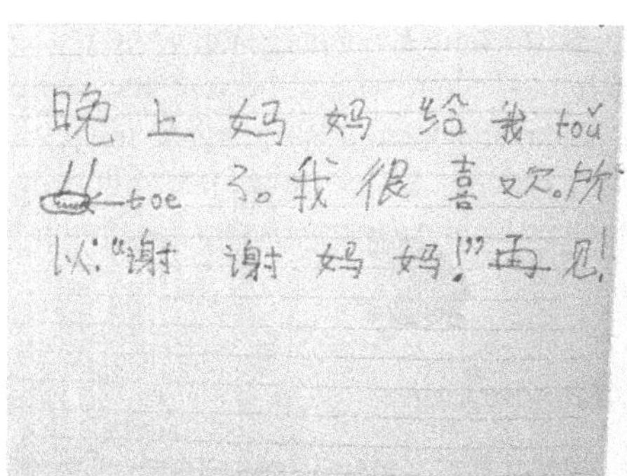

FIGURE 3.5 Code-switching (6:9) [In the evening, Mom painted my toes. I like (it) very much. So, "Thanks, mom!" Goodbye!]

At times, CoCo wrote entire English sentences only to show her emotion of excitement:

> "My gcsh! This is grat! [My gosh! This is great!]"
> "Good luck, Fingers crossed!"
> "明天是 [tomorrow is] feild [field] trip to XXX state forest!!!"
> "I even got merry Christmas from the police driver!"

Occasionally, CoCo wrote one entire paragraph in English, so she did not have to pause for unfamiliar words that hindered and stopped her writing flow. The reason was that she could spell English words using her phonetic knowledge; however, Chinese is logographic, so she could not write from the pronunciation. CoCo generally wrote the main content in Chinese and the supplementary sections in English, reflecting her understanding that journaling was meant for her Chinese language practice while she was more familiar with English comprehension exercises from school. For example, CoCo often wrote interactive questions in English at the end of entries, "Do you like hot pot?" Then she gave two options to circle: "No. Yes." She also incorporated English in her illustrations.

Borrowing English Syntax in Chinese

Although CoCo wrote in Chinese, her sentence structures sometimes reflected English grammatical influence due to syntactical differences between Chinese and English. For example,

> "..., Couch K 说在 P.E. 课。[Coach K said in P.E. class, ...]"
> The correct sentence order in Chinese would be:
> Coach K 在 P.E. 课说 ... [Coach K in P.E. said, ...]
> Similarly, in Figure 3.6, CoCo wrote:
> "你可以画画在石头上。[You can draw on the rocks.]"
> The proper Chinese sentence structure is:
> 你可以在石头上画画。[You can on the rocks draw.]

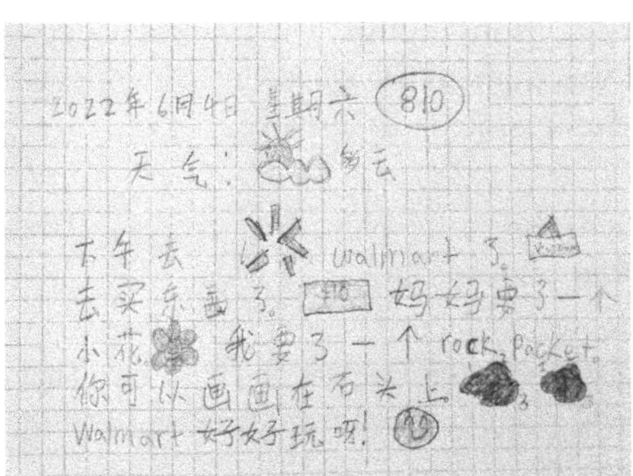

FIGURE 3.6 Shopping at Walmart (7:2)

CoCo inserted English adjectives for some description into Chinese sentences while retaining the Chinese adjective marker "的" in the sentence, as seen in:

"fake 的草" (fake + adjective marker+ grass)
"长 curly 的头发" (long curly + adjective marker + hair)

When incorporating only the English verbs in the Chinese sentence context, CoCo did not conjugate them. It could be that the Chinese language uses a separate character as a tense marker, "了" instead:

"win 了一个 prize [won one prize]"
"都 ignore 了 我 [all ignored me]"

However, when CoCo adopted the complete English sentence, she applied proper verb tenses:

"We explored the whole museum!"
"After school, 我和 Lulu were 朋友 again [Lulu and I were friends again after school]."

CoCo sometimes paid attention to the past tense when she borrowed English words.

"她 baked 一个 cake [She baked a cake.]"

She consistently kept a focus on past tense, either using English past tense or Chinese past tense marker or both.

"我 took 了五十一 min 和三十二 sec。[I took 51 minutes and 32 seconds.]"

She used both the past tense of "took" and "了." Additionally, she did not use plural forms for "minute" and "second." In Chinese, word nouns do not have the exact plural change as in English. The Chinese language uses numbers to indicate the plural form. Sometimes, when CoCo mentioned the plural forms in English, she added the -s ending, for instance,

"我需要做 tecnicol things 和 play 四个 pieces。[I need to do technical things and play four pieces.]"

Some expressions differ between English and Chinese. That means when CoCo translated the sentence word by word from English to Chinese, it did not make sense. For example,

"他要拿 Door。[He wants to hold the door.]"

The appropriate way to express it in Chinese is:

他要扶着门。

The common word-to-word translation of *hold* is 拿; however, this context in the example needs a different Chinese word. Another example is:

"我爸爸给我弄早，我妈妈给我弄晚。" [My dad got me (to school early, and my mom got me to school late.]

CoCo seemed to translate the sentence from English to Chinese. A more natural Chinese phrasing would be:

我爸爸很早送我来（学校），我妈妈很晚送我来（学校）。[My dad sends me to school early, my mom sends me to school late.]

Using English Phonetics to Sound Out Chinese Words

In first grade, CoCo sounded out English words and associated the sound with the visuals when she wrote them. She spelled:

"Pnceiess" for *princess*,
"Gama" for *grandma*,
"Tik-or-tet" for *trick-or-treat*,
"younconn" for *unicorn*,
"Crissmas" for *Christmas*, and
"flowshot" for *flu shot*.

However, Chinese is a Tibetan language that cannot be written out by sound (see more about the Chinese language in Chapter 1). When writing in Chinese, CoCo mixed up some words. She missed or added one stroke in Chinese characters and reversed two parts within one character or two characters within one word. When she relied on the sound, she miswrote the homophones. Also, she relied on the graphics and wrote words that looked similar but carried different meanings.

The Chinese phonetic system is pinyin (see more in Chapter 1). Many pinyin letters are the same as English letters. CoCo attempted to use pinyin for unknown Chinese words. However, CoCo did not learn pinyin systematically or know the correct rules. Therefore, she chose English phonetics and Chinese intonation for marking new Chinese words. While English does not have any tone changes,

Chinese has four different tones to mark intonation changes. For example, she spelled:

> "byǎw yǎn [biǎo yǎn]" for 表演 [performance],
> "lày [lèi]" for 累 [tired], and
> "dày 口 zhòw [dài 口 zhào]" for 戴口罩 [wear a face mask].
> Chapter 2 describes a similar confusion in her reading.

Including Spanish as an Additional Language

CoCo began learning Spanish in kindergarten (see Chapter 5) and occasionally mentioned her Spanish learning experiences in her journal. She even incorporated some Spanish words, for instance, "cero [zero]" and "inglés [English]." Additionally, she wrote "Merry Christmas" in three languages when she was seven. In her illustration of Spanish-speaking workers digging holes in our front yard for installing an internet cable, CoCo blended Spanish, Chinese, and English and even gave fake Spanish names to the workers (see Figure 3.7), demonstrating her ability to engage with her full linguistic repertoire.

FIGURE 3.7 Illustration in Three Languages (8:3)

Multimodality

When we first started to journal at the age of five, I often used different colors or designed the texts in creative ways to engage CoCo and encouraged her participation. For example, when she narrated her strawberry-picking experience, I arranged the text in a strawberry shape using three colors. I used a blue color pen for time, a green color, and a red color for her narration. In the first two journal books, I drew some simple illustrations (e.g., hot pot, banana, heart, stars) while CoCo doodled her name, the date, or sometimes filled the entire page with drawings. She also traced one sentence using a different color ink pen and demonstrated the steps to write simple Chinese characters. Additionally, she drew a text frame using red-colored lines, circled words, and illustrated my writing. When she transitioned to writing in lined journal books, CoCo initially wrote Chinese characters across two lines due to the narrow space between the lines (see Figure 3.5). Since Chinese characters are logographic and written next to each other without spaces in between, except for punctuation marks, I introduced her to graph composition books and graph ruled sheets with grids (see Figure 3.6) resembling Tianzige, the Chinese character writing practice sheet with square blocks. These allowed her to fit the characters neatly within the square blocks using a pencil. Throughout her journal entries, CoCo consistently incorporated multiple modes. She used illustrations for different purposes, designed text features, and borrowed mixed media to enrich her storytelling.

Illustrations

CoCo relied on illustrations regardless of her ability to write the Chinese characters. Her drawings sometimes reiterated the text content, added supplementary details, or functioned as stand-alone storylines. She also integrated text within her illustrations.

CoCo frequently illustrated her journal entries by depicting objects or events from her writing. While her text could be understood independently, her drawings added decorative or expressive elements. For example, she illustrated the Walmart logo, a flower, and rocks that were mentioned in her writing in Figure 3.6. In another example, when describing an encounter with a coyote in a park, she drew the animal. Similarly, when she wrote her first camping trip, CoCo illustrated a mountain, a vineyard, and marshmallows on sticks that she depicted in her texts. Other examples include a swan egg in the park with its measurement, her report card, and astronaut gloves at a community Science, Technology, Engineering, and Mathematics (STEM) event. At age six and a half, CoCo wrote a song about a flower and illustrated the yellow sun, a cloud with a blue outline, a pink flower, and green grass that were mentioned in her lyrics.

Beyond decoration, CoCo used both text and illustrations to convey meaning, and the illustrations added supplementary information (see Figure 3.5). For example, she sketched a cell in orange and yellow along with the experiment steps of observing a cell under a microscope. She also used drawings to replace the unknown words. In one entry, unsure how to write the word "tent," she drew a tent instead. Additionally, CoCo included graphs, charts, and bullet lists in her journal. For instance, she made a chart to show the number of girls and boys for a beach trip. Last, CoCo embedded emojis in the text and at the beginning of the journal to convey emotions in her journal book 5 (e.g., happy, sad, supprized [surprised], excited).

In her most recent journal book, CoCo sketched a storyline in her illustrations beyond the text. Some of those illustrations align with the content of the text, and some serve as independent stories similar to comic book panels. For example, she drew the school theater space and the car riders waiting to be picked up after school, the assistant principal and a few girls talking about ladybugs on the playground during recess, and children playing chess in the after-school club.

Within her illustrations, CoCo often embedded texts within the pictures for dialoging, thinking, labeling, captioning, and providing additional information. Influenced by her love for picture books and graphic novels, she frequently used speech bubbles and wrote texts within for conversations between her and her teacher and among girls at her school. She also used speech bubbles for different scenes in her stories. CoCo labeled various objects in her pictures to provide supplementary information, such as a birdhouse, parts of a flower, violin parts, and a map. Additionally, she labeled the steps of opening a lunch box and a flow chart. In Figure 3.8, CoCo diagrammed the cycle of a pumpkin in both Chinese and English and titled her picture at age eight. All those examples demonstrated her ability to present the text features effectively in her journals.

Text Design

Even when composing solely in text, CoCo designed and created new ways to arrange and edit her compositions. Before transitioning to writing in the graph composition sheets with a pencil, CoCo experimented with a variety of colors in her journal. She colored the words and titles, traced words, doodled, and decorated characters. Additionally, she alternated colors word-by-word or paragraph-by-paragraph.

CoCo also explored various text layouts. For example, she drew text blocks, drew a letter frame, and arranged the text in the shape of a strawberry. She wrote texts in different directions and adopted different font sizes. To ensure she wrote Chinese characters neatly in the same size, CoCo employed tiny dots to separate words and organize the layout for one entry. She used all capitalized letters

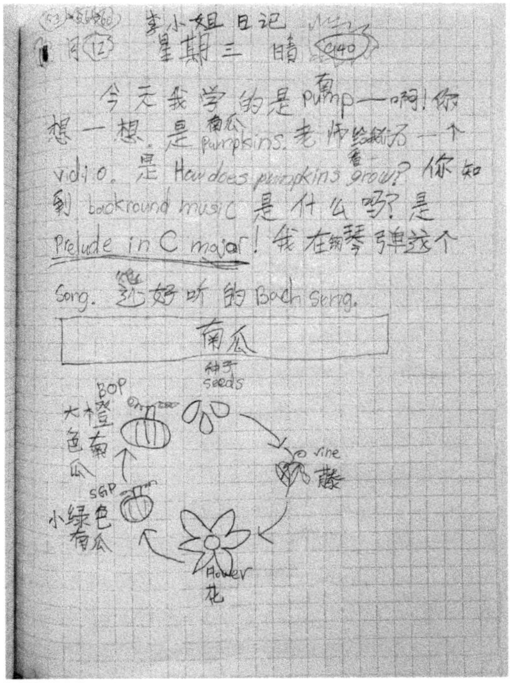

FIGURE 3.8 Journal about the Cycle of a Pumpkin (8:0)

to indicate titles and names. Although capitalization doesn't exist in Chinese writing, she enlarged some Chinese words to show her emotions and emphasis. Within the text, CoCo incorporated arrows to point the reading direction. For example, she applied an orange line to connect all the words, arrows to point at certain words, and an orange arrow to point at the bottom right corner, indicating the continuation of the journal. CoCo sometimes numbered the paragraphs and the sentences and included word count. In her journals, she practiced cursive writing and designed artistic letters.

In her writing, CoCo frequently used punctuation marks and special marks for clarity and emphasis. She learned to apply parentheses for explanations, for instance, explaining word meanings in parentheses with a different color, adding names for people mentioned, writing Chinese words by pinyin, and inserting hyperlinks. She inserted quotation marks, carets, and @. CoCo also highlighted, circled, and underlined some texts like transitional words and headings. Beginning using colored pens at the age of six, she could not erase miswritten words, so I shared a trick that I did back in high school, which was drawing a heart to block the miswritten word. Therefore, CoCo adopted this practice to cover the crossed-out words using hearts and a variety of icons, such as hearts, red balloons, blueberries, and suns, often themed to match her journal topics. For example, in Figure 3.3, CoCo designed tooth drawings to cover the miswritten word in her note to the tooth fairy. Her text design was associated with her meaning-making. Another alternative for covering her mistakes was that CoCo used arrows over the miswritten words to connect the sentences.

Mixed Media

In addition to colors, colored pens, pencils, varied text fonts, multiple languages, and illustrations, CoCo utilized other media available in her journal. For example, she put up many stickers (e.g., hearts, stars, letters) and added stickers that she received from attending events, such as a Japanese name tag from an International Festival and a birthday sticker from a party. Interestingly, in one journal entry about learning paper cutout window flowers (6:4), CoCo cut a small red window flower, wrote the Chinese character "窗 [window]" on it, and pasted it on the page. The Chinese window flowers are cut out from red paper because red symbolizes fortune in Chinese culture. This reflects that CoCo integrated her linguistic, cultural, and multimodal knowledge in creating her journal. Later, in another journal, CoCo taped a note slip that she wrote at school and embedded it as part of her journal entry. Taken together, those examples show that living in a multimodal world, CoCo borrowed the designs, colors, and text forms from her surroundings and invented her own multimodal compositions.

Cultural Connections

It is worth noting that CoCo's journal entries reflect her engagement with heritage culture, living in mixed cultures, and maintaining transnational relationships.

Heritage Culture

Heritage cultural connections are highlighted in CoCo's journals. She documented traditional Chinese holiday celebrations such as the Lunar New Year, Lantern Festival, Dragonboat Festival, Mid-Autumn Festival, and 腊八节 [Laba Festival, the eighth day of the 12th lunar month]. She also wrote her presentation of the Lunar New Year in her third-grade classroom at school. Additionally, she wrote the seasons and solar terms in the Chinese lunar calendar, 二十四节气, for example, 春分 [Vernal Equinox], 清明 [Clear and Bright], 小暑 [Slight Heat], 小雪 [Light Snow], and 冬至 [Winter Solstice]. Figure 3.2 shows her two journal entries about the Mid-Autumn Festival from 2020 and 2021, where she wrote about and illustrated this holiday's traditions. On the left, she described, "Tonight, my mom and I watched the Mid-Autumn Festival gala (on TV), which was great!" She also drew flowers in a vase, grapes that people often ate for this festival, and video conferencing on my phone with her lǎolao in China. We celebrated virtually since we could not do it in person together for this family reunion festival. CoCo used circles as the placeholders of the Chinese characters that she could not write and asked me to fill in. In her journal a year later, on the right side, she wrote an expository text titled Mid-Autumn Day, introducing this festival and its celebration as below:

> The Mid-Autumn Festival is August 15th. On the Mid-Autumn Festival, we all eat mooncakes. When eating mooncakes, (we can) also look at the moon. Families celebrate this festival together. Some also hang lanterns. Some can even go to bed later.
>
> *[translated from Figure 3.2]*

CoCo marked her emotion of the day as "I am happy" with a smiley face emoji and a self-portrait. In her illustration of the festival nighttime picnic, she sat with her parents and one close friend around the table with mooncakes and appreciated the moon in the sky. She specified that this piece was written and illustrated by her with her Chinese name "李师杨 [Shiyang Li]" and "6 岁 [age of six]."

Moreover, CoCo wrote about Chinese icons and cultural objects, such as the dragon, the Chinese zodiac, the Year of the Ox, red envelopes, Tai chi, and guzheng—a Chinese plucked string instrument. For instance, she wrote a story about Emperor Qin building the Great Wall and included other television programs, festival galas, shows, and YouTube videos introducing Chinese culture. CoCo's journals also featured various Chinese foods. For instance, she wrote and illustrated hot pot eight times, fall dumplings, spring rolls, multi-grain porridge, and seasonal holiday food such as moon cake and 粽子 [sticky rice dumplings]. For her birthday wish, CoCo wrote, "明年我生日想回中国吃个冰糖葫芦 [I wanted to go to China and eat candied hawthorns for my birthday next year] (5:2)." Candied hawthorns on sticks are popular winter snacks in the north of Mainland China that I grew up with and introduced to her.

Names carry family culture and important meanings for Chinese people. CoCo wrote about her Chinese name and her Chinese birthday following the Chinese lunar calendar. I helped her write our extended family members' names in Chinese in one of the journal entries. Additionally, CoCo wrote about the birth of her niece and a cousin and their names. She compiled a bullet list of facts about China and named it "我眼里的中国 [China in my eyes] (5:5)." In a separate entry, CoCo drew a Chinese dress with "福 [fortune]" on the front and "中华人民共和国 [People's Republic of China]" and stars on the sleeves. In the letter "给善良的好妈妈 [To (My) Kind and Nice Mother]" in Figure 3.9, she drew me wearing a dress with China's national flag and the word "中国 [China]" on it and her in a dress with the word "美国 [the United States]" and the flag of the United States. In the picture, I was holding a bag of "中国种子 [Chinese seeds]," and she was watering the flowers that grew from the seeds.

FIGURE 3.9 Letter to Mom (7:9)

This picture and her journal indicate CoCo's identities as a daughter and an American-born Chinese child.

Mixed Cultures

In addition to Chinese culture, CoCo wrote about American holidays and events and activities on those holidays, such as a New Year's Eve celebration, Valentine's Day, St. Patrick's Day, Easter and egg hunting, the Fourth of July fireworks, Labor Day and its parade, carving a pumpkin and trick-or-treating on Halloween, Election Day, Thanksgiving, our family Christmas tree, and Santa's visit.

Furthermore, CoCo mixed Chinese and American cultures in her journals because these Western and Eastern cultures were both parts of her identity. For example, our family celebrated both American and Chinese holidays. The Chinese New Year, aka the Spring Festival, is often in late January or early February. In 2021, we left the Christmas tree up after New Year's Day and replaced ornaments with red Chinese lucky knots for the Spring Festival decoration. CoCo recorded this special decoration of mixed cultures. Additionally, Valentine's Day and the Lantern Festival overlapped in 2022, so CoCo included both days in one journal entry and embellished with red hearts as well as red lanterns. Also, Easter is usually around the same time as 清明, the Tomb Sweeping Day—the Chinese memorial day for ancestors and past family members. CoCo drew decorations for both days in one entry. Interestingly, even when she wrote notes to the Tooth Fairy, she mixed two languages (see Figure 3.3). Overall, these examples indicate her mixed identity as a Chinese American.

Transnational Relationship and Global Awareness

CoCo's embrace of Chinese culture is through family and the virtual connection to families in China during the COVID-19 pandemic. She journaled about talking via an online conferencing app with her grandparents, aunts and uncles, cousins, one little niece, and friends. Those family members and friends live in different places in China, and one family lives in England. Occasionally, CoCo had virtual playdates with them. For example, she drew pictures with a friend who lived in China and sang and danced with her aunt who lived in England. CoCo also played cards and mahjong—a Chinese tile-based game with lǎolao (see Figure 1.4) and held live-stream piano and violin concerts for our Chinese relatives. After learning that she would visit China in the summer of 2023, CoCo wrote her plan for the China trip and drew herself flying in an airplane to China. Furthermore, she recorded her conversation with a friend from South Korea about each of their summer plans, which was visiting their respective home countries (8:7). Following that in the same journal entry, CoCo drew a Chinese national flag and wrote that the last time she visited was in 2019, before the COVID-19 pandemic. Her transnational relationship and immigrant friends around her helped her gain global awareness and her identity.

CoCo documented her global awareness and the diverse cultures that she interacted with in her journals. Living in a global context, she showed her knowledge of the time difference between China and the U.S. CoCo wrote about our family's friends' struggles with traveling back to China during the pandemic. She wrote the pretend game of traveling to London that included preparing a passport, doing custom checks, boarding, sightseeing, and visiting her aunt. She wrote about watching the World Cup, the Summer Olympics, and the Winter Olympics on television. In addition to an international perspective, CoCo expressed her intercultural awareness by writing about her diverse local community. For instance, she attended a local event, the International Festival, where she received her Japanese name card and learned ikebana, a Japanese flower arrangement. Additionally, CoCo wrote that she explored the country of South Korea as her cultural project at school. She also included Japanese poems and art that she learned from school, her ice-skating coach's Russian name, her name in Korean that she learned from the language table—a weekly language conversation practice on a university campus, Mexican food, and

Spanish-speaking workers that she met in the neighborhood. Overall, CoCo's journals reflect a growing intercultural awareness and an evolving identity as a Chinese American and a global citizen in a multicultural world.

Discussion

As a bilingual writer, CoCo engaged in multiple languages, employed multimodality, and created multiple genres in her journal practice. She utilized a range of semiotic resources—Chinese characters, pinyin, English, Spanish, and pictures—to design her journals, create meaning, develop writing fluency, and cultivate independence. Through this family-supported journal writing process, she shaped her identity as an author while also reinforcing her linguistic and cultural identities. This practice requires intentional family commitment, scaffolding, and an embracement of both cultures.

Using Languages for Pragmatic Purposes

Our experience shows that family multilingual journal writing is a significant endeavor demanding extensive modeling, guidance, and encouragement. Translanguaging played a central role in CoCo's language learning and took commitment. It is very common for bilingual speakers to borrow words from another language spontaneously and pragmatically for communication (Baker, 2014). Baker (2014) stated, "Children naturally use both languages to maximize learning. Children are pragmatists, and use both of their languages to amplify understanding and enhance language performance in the street and school (p. 206)." CoCo's journal entries demonstrated that she possessed one holistic linguistic pool, and she selected the codes efficiently for her purpose. For example, she seamlessly alternated between English and Chinese words, blended syntactic structures from both languages, used English phonetics to sound out Chinese words, and even embedded Spanish words, all contributing to the same purpose of expressing herself. As CoCo simultaneously developed proficiency in two languages, her languages and cultures were not half this and half that. Her bilingual and cultural affiliation was fluid (Cunningham, 2020). She used her full linguistic repertoire in her writing. CoCo's learning of Spanish expanded her linguistic repertoire, allowing her to experiment with three languages. The findings suggest that her language choices were driven by personal needs and convenience, reinforcing the idea that multilingual learners pragmatically leverage their full linguistic resources.

In alignment with the benefits of translanguaging in previous research (Baker & Wright 2021; García & Li, 2014; García et al., 2017), CoCo's translanguaging not only enhanced her motivation to learn but also deepened her meaning and understanding, greater metalinguistic awareness, linguistic consciousness, and sociolinguistic consciousness. Her translanguaging also affirmed her bilingual identities and devotion to greater social interaction, communication, and empowerment. Furthermore, translanguaging contributed to her meaning-making, writing fluency, and confidence boost as a writer. It helped her see that writing is a joyful process instead of encoding using a single language system. The observations provide further support for the idea that multilingual children use their full linguistic repertoire and symbols for meaning-making. Meanwhile, CoCo's linguistic knowledge grew as she practiced her journal writing.

Developing Multimodal and Multigenre Writing

Through the journaling practice, CoCo progressively developed her heritage language writing proficiency. Through the gradual release of responsibility (Fisher & Frey, 2013), she grew from narrating her journal to writing with support and, ultimately, to independent writing. Dictating children's stories plays a critical role in their writing development, and it is important to maintain consistency in writing practice and language development (Wang, 2008). Writing in their home languages gives children a tool to represent and process their experiences (Wang, 2008).

Along with the improvement of writing conventions, CoCo developed strong authorship. An intriguing observation was CoCo's tendency to communicate with an imagined readership in her journal, fostering an interactive writing style. A possible explanation for this phenomenon might be attributed to the influence of her reading experiences, which introduced her to different genres and textual conventions. In an 11-year observation of her two children developing three languages simultaneously, Wang (2008) used free drawing to help her children express themselves. Similarly, in CoCo's journal, her freedom to use multigenre and multimodality boosted her self-confidence in using her home language and helped her express herself. CoCo demonstrated ownership of her journal writing and identity formation as a multilingual multimodal writer.

Research has established that L2 reading develops L2 writing skills (Baker, 2014). CoCo's case exemplifies how reading multigenre and multimodal texts enriched her writing style, nurtured her writing development, and cultivated her writer identity. CoCo explicitly reflected on her bilingual reading experiences in her journal, noting that she "love(d) reading" and believed that "reading is making predictions, thinking."

The texts CoCo read clearly served as mentor texts that influenced her writing style. For example, the *Owl Diaries Series* (Elliott, 2015–2020), known for its interactive dialogues and vibrant illustrations, inspired CoCo to incorporate conversational elements in her journal entries. Similarly, her exposure to *Xiaopipa* (n.d.)—a Chinese children's magazine, led her to adopt formatting features such as numbering the paragraphs and sentences and to list the author's name, illustrator's name, and her age underneath the title. She also learned to add the author's biographies and fact text boxes from reading children's literature books. After reading fables, she began adding moral lessons learned at the end of her journal entries. By third grade, her fascination with graphic novels influenced her to embed comic panels into her journal, while Chinese anthologies enriched her linguistic expression. Apparently, the aforementioned books became her mentor texts. These literary influences reinforced the idea that children's reading experiences directly shape their writing styles and authorial identities.

Despite the act of writing being a multimodal practice (Kenner, 2003), CoCo used multiple semiotic resources in her journal (Jewitt, 2008; Kress, 2011). Multimodality helped her convey meaning and cultivated her authorship. Her use of drawing, visual support of the pictures and colors, allowed her to add to the linguistic output that she wrote in the journal. The mode CoCo selected, such as writing or pictures, carried important meanings for her. When the printed text was insufficient for representing her meaning, she relied on drawing and choices of pen color to convey meaning at the word and sentence levels—and overall. CoCo did not keep her languages or modes in separate boxes; rather, she fluidly shuffled between them, selecting the most effective means of expression for each context. In this sense, bilingual children are pragmatists, too.

Forming Multiple Identities

Children's "identities constantly develop and change, across time and across situations." (Baker & Wright, 2021, p. 137). CoCo's journaling was a family investment in her language and cultural identities (Darvin & Norton, 2015; Norton, 2013; 2018). Her journals captured her active multilingual multicultural identity development processes. Through journaling, she interpreted her daily experiences, feelings, emotions, thoughts, and developments in daily narratives (Wang, 2008). Additionally, Baker and Wright (2021) found that other community members and situations created and confined children's identities. In this case, CoCo constructed her identities, and her identities were constructed by her interaction with family members, her negotiating with other social members, and her writing.

CoCo identified herself through writing, and she accessed her funds of knowledge (González et al., 2005; Moll, 2014) from her mixed cultural reservoir. She identified her name, her languages, her cultures, and being a global citizen. CoCo wrote Chinese holidays in the Chinese language and her New Year's resolution in English, which indicates her association with languages and cultures. Her journals show her Chinese heritage culture, American culture, and the blended culture that she lived with. Although she compared and contrasted those two cultures, journaling and conversations around the content cultivated her sense of belonging to both cultures. In writing her journal, CoCo embraced her cultural heritage, lived through mixed cultures in the United States, and built transnational connections. Furthermore, her journaling expanded beyond Chinese and American cultures to include influences from Korean and Latinx cultures, reinforcing her development of intercultural and global awareness and forming her global citizen identity.

Family Scaffolding, Celebration, and Commitment

Parental support plays a vital role in children's multilingual development (Baker & Wright, 2021; Wang, 2008) and parents should create opportunities to talk with children to scaffold their home language development (Wang, 2008). The four phases of CoCo's journaling illustrate my gradual release of responsibility as a parent (Fisher & Frey, 2013). It is critical for children to access role models and mentor texts to follow. Additionally, I shared my journal writing experiences when I was a child and a college student with CoCo. We checked out journal-style books from the library to read and discuss the different features of those journal books. We read Anne Frank's diary and biography. Her father stepped in and did the same when I had work obligations. He joined us in writing his journal for a while. As parents, we provided writing role models by demonstrating this routine, writing persistence, neat handwriting, and writing clarity for CoCo, and we regarded journal writing as family time together. One unanticipated result was that journaling became a family time of sharing, learning, and reflecting.

In addition to journaling, we sometimes read journals aloud. When CoCo started to write by herself, she used mixed codes (Chinese words, pinyin, English, and visuals), some of which only made sense to her. Then, I asked her to read the journal aloud after she had written and recorded it with a video camera on a device. CoCo loved seeing herself in the videos and reading to an imagined audience. Furthermore, we often video chatted with my mother and our relatives and friends around the same time, so CoCo read aloud or shared her journals with them when discussing her life. Additionally, her journal book became the spotlight item of her show-and-share sessions at school, reinforcing the social value of her writing. In her first-grade virtual class, CoCo shared her journal books with her teacher and the entire class. She mentioned that she wanted to publish her journal books, just like Anne Frank. More than that, we started numbering the journal entries on the first day that we sheltered at home because of the COVID-19 pandemic. When it reached 100, we celebrated with a homemade cake with "100" icing on it. Then, we celebrated those mini-milestones every 100 days, a tradition that continued through 1,200 entries.

Despite journal writing being a family commitment, we did have our struggles. We gradually found that the time before bed worked the best. Therefore, we often wrote over nighttime snacks. Our office supplies and dictionaries were available beside our table. CoCo had to make up her journals when we traveled. Sometimes, she wanted us to develop a few pieces into formal writing pieces, such as a book review and a memoir, instead of a usual journal. This multilingual family writing project has its limitations. Given that the initial aim was for CoCo to practice her heritage language and take ownership of her writing, her Chinese characters and English writing imperfections, grammatical inconsistencies, and conventional inaccuracies were not all corrected. Some variations were pointed out when they affected the meaning critically. Her writing products were mostly embraced and celebrated as evidence of her self-efficacy and growth mindset. Furthermore, as a single case study, the findings may not be fully generalized to other multilingual learners because not all children are the same, and the impact across languages may be different, too.

Implications

This journal writing practice suggests to researchers that multilingual writers can employ language pragmatically and use all semiotic resources to convey meaning and negotiate their identities in their writing. More exploration can be conducted to investigate family commitment in multilingual children's writing practices and to explore the intersections of meaning-making using multiple languages and mixed modes.

For educators, implementing multilingual writing workshops (Laman, 2013) and writing conferences (Espinosa & Ascenzi-Moreno, 2021) can create inclusive spaces for children to write multilingual journals and use the languages that they prefer. Teachers can also encourage multilingual children to use different modes to design their products. When assessing children's writing, teachers can apply a generous reading approach—reading holistically with an open mind—and value multilingual children's strengths (Spence, 2014). Lastly, parents and community partners can foster more opportunities and spaces for multilingual children to write and create with their languages as much as they can. Journal writing may look different in different families. There is no need to set up a goal of writing 1,000 journals. Teachers and parents can model writing to multilingual children, for instance, by drafting an email, making a grocery list, editing a text message or a social media post, and writing a family letter. Ultimately, nurturing multilingual writers and global citizens requires a collaborative effort from families, educators, and the broader community.

Inquiry Questions

Questions for Researchers:

- How do multilingual children develop their multiple identities through writing practice?
- How can family members contribute to their children's bilingual writing practices?

Questions for Teachers:

- What instructional strategies can teachers employ to cultivate bilingual authorship?
- How can teachers access children's funds of knowledge and linguistic repertoire in teaching writing?

Questions for Parents:

- What strategies could parents employ to foster their children's heritage language writing at home?
- How can bilingual parents support their children's bilingual writing development?
- What community resources are available for bilingual children's writing development?

Suggested Reading

Espinosa, C. M., & Ascenzi-Moreno, L. (2021). *Rooted in strength: Using translanguaging to grow multilingual readers and writers*. Scholastic.

Fu, D. (2009). *Writing between languages: How English language learners make the transition to fluency*. Heinemann.

Laman, T. T. (2013). *From ideas to words: Writing strategies for English language learners*. Heinemann.

Spence, L. (2014). *Student writing: Give it a generous reading*. Information Age Publishing.

4

BOOKS, DISCUSSION, AND ARTIFACTS

Reading and Responding to Bilingual and Bicultural Children's Literature Books

Yang Wang & Ling Hao

This chapter describes CoCo's bilingual and bicultural development at home in conjunction with a virtual community-based, culturally relevant book club led by Dr. Ling Hao during the COVID-19 pandemic. At that time, I was seeking additional opportunities for CoCo to engage with a broader community beyond her virtual school class. Dr. Ling Hao was a volunteer teacher at a local heritage language school and a doctoral candidate with whom I collaborated closely. Starting in the spring of 2021, Ling held a community-based virtual bilingual family book club for a group of Chinese American families. This initiative aimed to promote the bilingual and bicultural development of Chinese American children and foster their understanding of their cultural heritage. As a result, CoCo and I participated in Ling's family book club.

Numerous previous studies have highlighted the crucial role of home literacy experiences and parental involvement in young children's bilingual development (Louie & Davis-Welton, 2016; Noguerón-Liu et al., 2020; Ryan, 2021). Parents' lived experiences significantly influence their children's home literacy development. Thus, it is important to understand how young children develop their biliterate skills in the home context (Li, 2006; Yang et al., 2021). Specifically, this chapter examines how CoCo employed a mesh of literacy experiences to make meaning of Chinese American and Chinese picturebooks, thereby shaping her bicultural identity within the home environment. The central research question is: How does a child develop bilingual and bicultural competencies through reading and responding to culturally relevant picturebooks in a virtual family book club?

International literature is books created by international authors and/or illustrators, featuring international characters or settings in international contexts,

DOI: 10.4324/9781003517061-4

whereas multicultural literature represents minority groups within the United States (Short, 2016). Both multicultural and international literature provide bilingual children with windows, mirrors, and sliding doors to learn about their cultural heritage, explore other cultures, and navigate their hybrid identities living within diverse communities in the United States (Bishop, 1990; Glazier & Seo, 2011). Culturally relevant literature and bilingual books play a vital role in helping bilingual readers develop literacy skills, construct cultural and linguistic identities, and foster critical consciousness (Osorio, 2018).

This chapter is informed by reader response theory (Rosenblatt, 1978/1994), funds of knowledge (González et al., 2005; Moll et al., 1992), and translanguaging (García & Li, 2014; Chapter 1). Readers bring their unique backgrounds as they transact with the texts, drawing on their cultural and linguistic background knowledge to make connections across literary works (Hao, 2023; Pu, 2010). Additionally, young children make meaning and respond to texts like picturebooks through multiple modes (Brown, 2021; Wohlwend et al., 2022), such as language, drawings, and body movements. Multimodal responses reflect the diverse ways in which young children engage with texts. Additionally, children leverage their funds of knowledge—readers' lived experience and their skills that are culturally and historically developed (Esteban & Moll, 2014; Moll et al., 1992; Newman, 2012) and their families' cultural practices to make sense of texts (Hao, 2023).

Translanguaging practices—leveraging language resources with flexibility and transcending traditional linguistic boundaries—can be one way to teach inclusively (Fu et al., 2019). Translanguaging practices can be viewed as multimodal processes to understand readers' meaning-making actions as they involve utilizing readers' full linguistic repertoires (Li, 2018). Through translanguaging practices, parents can share family histories and cultural heritage with their children. Research suggests that bilingual families utilize their full linguistic resources to support bilingual development (Moody et al., 2021; Yang et al., 2021). Some families use translanguaging during shared readings to facilitate translations and predictions (Song, 2016). Moody and colleagues (2021) explored a bilingual parent's translanguaging practices during shared read-alouds and found that the parent engaged in translanguaging for different purposes, such as prompting the child to recall and summarize the stories. Bilingual families also utilize translanguaging practices to support reading comprehension. For example, Yang and her colleagues (2021) explored a Chinese American bilingual family's conversational interactions during book readings. They found that the family utilized translanguaging at the vocabulary and sentence levels to support two young children's comprehension. Previous studies have shown that young bilingual children employ translanguaging practices to develop their biliteracy skills (Brown, 2016; Perry et al., 2008). This chapter highlights CoCo's language negotiation processes as she discussed culturally relevant picturebooks and created multimodal responses to these picturebooks.

Methodology

The ethnographic case study method (Compton-Lilly, 2021) was employed for a detailed analysis of CoCo's multimodal reading responses to bilingual children's books. This method provided an in-depth understanding of her bilingual and bicultural development, allowing for the identification of emerging patterns within the data.

The family book club sessions were conducted via Zoom, an online video conferencing platform, for the convenience of the participants during the COVID-19 pandemic. A total of six families from the Southeast, Northeast, and Midwest regions of the United States participated, meeting via Zoom every Sunday morning for one year. CoCo and I participated as one family dyad. The book club sessions were held in two languages and spanned 28 meetings (18 sessions in the spring and ten sessions in the fall), each lasting approximately 90 minutes.

Ling introduced Chinese American literature and Chinese literature to the children and their families in the book club, reading one book per session. Ling and I discussed selecting authentic contemporary Chinese American picturebooks and international picturebooks created by authors and illustrators from the insider group or Mainland China, following the criteria of representing Chinese culture, carrying daily experiences that Chinese American children can relate to, and being in Mandarin Chinese, English, or both. Approximately 60% of the books selected were published in English, 25% in Chinese, and 15% were bilingual books. All books were authored or illustrated by at least one Chinese or Chinese American creator (see children's literature cited). Topics included heritage culture, holidays, family histories, family relationships, intergenerational relationships, seasonal events, food, and cultural artifacts. Most of the books were fictional stories, with two being color and shape books.

Each family book club session followed a structured four-part format. First, Ling read the selected book aloud in two languages. She translated the monolingual books into Mandarin when necessary. Ling paused her reading after each page to allow sufficient time for children and parents to read the texts on their own, examine the illustrations, and comprehend the characters, the settings, and the plots. Following the read-aloud, Ling posed a few discussion prompts (e.g., connections to heritage culture, family traditions) for family dyads to explore. Next, children designed multimodal artifacts to express their interpretations of the book and build heritage cultural connections with their parents. Finally, children shared their artifacts with the larger group. CoCo eagerly volunteered to present her creations at each session.

Primary data sources included audio recordings of CoCo's family book discussions, her multimodal artworks, and descriptions of her artifacts in each session. Supplementary data comprised Zoom video recordings of group activities and photographs of CoCo's home work space (i.e., table and office supplies).

The book discussions were transcribed and analyzed through open coding (Stake, 1995) to identify CoCo's responses to texts. Discourse analysis (Gee, 2014) was borrowed to analyze her language use. CoCo's artifacts and descriptions were analyzed through content analysis (Miles et al., 2020) to identify modality, cultural aspects, and linguistic aspects. Finally, Ling and I synthesized the coded data to identify major thematic patterns. The next section presents three key findings.

Findings

In this family book club, CoCo developed bicultural identities via reading and responding to culturally relevant bilingual picturebooks. First, through the discussion about the picturebooks with Ling, other children, and me, CoCo negotiated her cultural identities. Second, CoCo adopted multiple modes, evidenced in the artifacts, to represent her evolving understanding of the books, her culture, and herself. Third, her bilingual practices meshed in the discussion and artifacts contributed to her linguistic identity.

Conferring Cultural Heritage

CoCo utilized her mesh of experiences to make meaning through our reading conferences during and after reading culturally relevant picturebooks. CoCo's identity development was deeply intertwined with her lived experience, her conversations with me, and our sharing of important cultural objects and traditions in our family.

Making Connections

CoCo's reading responses revealed her strong personal and cultural connections to the picturebooks and her family's funds of knowledge. She constantly shared her interests in the cultural components mentioned in the books and compared herself to the main characters. For instance, after reading *Celebrating the Lantern Festival* (Tang, 2010), CoCo enthusiastically stated, "我喜欢跟 dragon 跳舞，舞龙。我喜欢拿那个 stick. [I like dancing with dragons, dragon dance. I like holding that stick.]" Immediately, CoCo added that she appreciated the visual support in the book, noting, "picture for me to understand" and "他们长得样子像中国。还有 vegetable，中文字。 [They look like China. And there are vegetable and Chinese characters (in the picture).]" CoCo related to those cultural components in the books.

CoCo also extended her connections beyond books to family events, family members, her skin color, language, and other prior knowledge. She observed similarities between herself and book characters, remarking, "(The main character)

像我 [looks like me]," and "头发颜色 [Hair color], skin color (look like me)." Furthermore, she related what she read to her knowledge about different time zones. For instance, during the read-aloud of *I Dream of Popo* (Blackburne, 2021), which talked about a girl who moved to the United States and made video calls with her grandmother in the evening of American time and in the morning of Taiwan time, CoCo volunteered to share with the group that "每天，我有可能会给我的姥姥姥爷打电话。 [Every day, I may call my grandparents.]" Her comment prompted other children to discuss their similar experiences of calling their grandparents or siblings who live in China, further reinforcing their shared cultural identity. Overall, CoCo's connections like these helped her reflect on her Chinese American identity and transnational experiences.

Expressing Curiosity

From our reading conference data, it is apparent that CoCo frequently asked many questions and expressed her curiosities about those books. She wondered about the authors' and illustrators' reasons for creating the books, the illustrations' reality, the text feature design, and the story setting. For example, CoCo wanted to ask the illustrator, Grace Lin, about her book *Red Is a Dragon: A Book of Colors* (Thong, 2008), "你为什么要做这个 color book? 和你是不是你自己做的? [Why did you make this color book? And did you make it by yourself?]" She also inquired about the author's linguistic background, "她会中文吗？应该会。（她）长得很像中国人。她会 Spanish 吗？[Does she know the Chinese language? Perhaps yes. (She) looks like Chinese. Does she know Spanish?]" Furthermore, CoCo's curiosity extended to cultural practices when she read about new cultural objects in picturebooks. For instance, she asked Ling to share her hometown's cuisine after learning that Ling was from the city mentioned in a book. Later, after reading *Father's Chinese Opera* (Lo, 2014), CoCo asked to watch Beijing Opera, a traditional performance that combines songs, instrumental music, martial arts, and dance. Similarly, *The Dragon Boat Festival and Glutinous Rice Dumplings* (Bao, 2021a) sparked her interest in making boats and learning more about Chinese dragons.

Moreover, CoCo discussed her wonders with other families of similar linguistic and cultural backgrounds. After reading *Thanking the Moon* (Lin, 2010), CoCo found that the Chinese American family in the book celebrated the Mid-Autumn Festival outdoors. CoCo questioned the setting of this story since the book introduced a Chinese holiday. She then proposed the question in the book club, "故事里的小朋友她们住在哪儿啊？ [Where do the children in the story live?]" Her question led to all the children's discussion about their different answers and reasons. While CoCo did not gather convincing evidence from the book or group discussion, she believed various interpretations could exist, highlighting the complexity of cultural identity.

Clarifying Confusion

CoCo cleared up the confusion about the fusion of Chinese and American cultures as we discussed the given books. For example, she generalized what we do in our family as Chinese culture; therefore, she assumed waffles were Chinese food because we ate waffles in our house. After reading a picturebook about a morning market in China—an open-air market with vendors selling local breakfast foods, fresh produce, meat, and other goods in the morning time, I introduced her to the evening market—an evening-time street market where people buy street food, souvenirs, clothing, crafts, and entertainments. CoCo had only been to the farmers market in the United States; thus, her interpretation of an evening market was selling "bed, blanket, pillow, toothbrush, sink." I explained that an evening market was similar to a morning market but held in the evening. Another cultural confusion was that after reading about Chinatown in a book, she predicted that Chinatown should be in China.

CoCo: 你去过 Chinatown 吗？ [Have you been to Chinatown?]
Yang: 去过。 [Yes.]
CoCo: 那你可不可以回中国带我去 Chinatown 啊？ [Then can you take me to Chinatown when we go to China?]
Yang: 咦， 我告诉你一个特别有意思的事啊。 Chinatown 不在中国在美国。 [Hey, let me tell you a very interesting thing. Chinatown is not in China but in the United States.]
CoCo: 啊？ 那它为什么？ [Ah? Why?]
Yang: 中国已经就是中国了啊。它不需要再有 Chinatown。 Chinatown 呢，是在世界其他国家和地区中国人的主要聚集地。 [China is just China. It does not need Chinatown. Chinatown is the main gathering place for Chinese people in other countries and regions around the world.]

CoCo initially assumed that anything related to China must exist only in China. The discussion helped her grasp the concept of Chinese diaspora communities. Learning about Chinatown helped her understand the book setting, the story, and Chinese American culture.

CoCo and other children associated language with culture, which could contribute to understanding their identities; however, it sometimes caused confusion. For example, CoCo thought this story in *What I Like Most* (Murphy, 2020) happens in the United States as she explained, "肯定不是中国，因为这本书是英文。 [It can't be in China, because this book is in English.]" After reading *Amy Wu and the Patchwork Dragon* (Zhang, 2020), CoCo commented, "她写中文字，就在中国。 [She writes Chinese characters, so she is in China.]" and "如果他们不知道中文他们怎么知道 Chinese culture 什么呀？ [If they don't know the Chinese language, how do they know what Chinese culture is?]" Through our discussion about the book, CoCo realized,

> (作者) 像我，因为她知道中文 and the culture, 她也知道英文。因为她两个都知道。东方龙知道，西方龙也知道。
>
> [(The author was) like me, because she knows Chinese and the culture, she also knows English. Because she knows both. She knows the eastern dragon and the western dragon.]

Talking about her unknowns and confusions helped her understand that culture is more than a language, and it also indicates that identity is complex.

Learning Traditions

As CoCo and I read and discussed Chinese American picturebooks, CoCo learned more about cultural traditions, home traditions, and variations of celebrations in different regions of China. For example, after reading about the Lantern Festival, CoCo noticed different celebrations in the book, which illustrated different types of lanterns from those in our house. Following her comment of "房子像 U.S.，没有赏月，lanterns 不一样。[The houses (in the book) are like those in the U.S. There is no moon appreciation. The lanterns are different.]" I shared other relevant traditions and variations of celebrations in different regions of China, such as different ways to make rice balls and various fillings for dumplings in the South and North of China. I also pointed out different Chinese operas other than the Beijing Opera mentioned in one book. Additionally, we compared Chinese festivals to American ones; for instance, Qingming—tomb-sweeping day in China and Easter were celebrated around the same time with spring outdoor activities. I shared that Chinese people developed new traditions nowadays to remember their ancestors on the day of Qingming.

CoCo viewed me as a cultural reference. During the read-aloud, she turned to me to ask questions and share cultural connections while reading picture books. For example, CoCo talked about our family's lived experience during the read-aloud of *The Dragon Boat Festival and Glutinous Rice Dumplings* (Bao, 2021a). She recalled that she made rice dumplings with her friend's family, and her father purchased rice dumplings from the Asian grocery store. Later, when she read that the main character added dates and sausages into the rice dumpling fillings, CoCo turned to me, pointed to the screen, and expressed her shock, "香肠 [sausages]!" because she only had plain sticky rice dumplings and those with dates and nuts but never had any with sausages. I confirmed the variety of rice dumpling filling choices. In this case, CoCo considered me a cultural reference and shared her connections and confusion with me.

We also talked about our home traditions. After reading the books in each session, I talked about some cultural connections, as those were my connections reading those books, and I wanted to take this chance to share our cultural heritage. Those connections helped CoCo develop her bicultural identities. For example, the name stamps were handed down from generation to generation in the family featured in *Grandfather's Stamp* (Hei, 2020). After reading, I shared with CoCo about our family members' stamps that were gifted from parents or grandparents. She then understood that each of our family members had a name stamp and began to be curious about the origin of these stamps. These discussions between the two of us showed that CoCo was aware of my cultural knowledge and used me as a resource in her own learning to support her heritage cultural development.

Designing Products

Along with discussing her connections, confusions, and traditions in the previous sections, CoCo responded by providing book reviews and actively incorporating her feedback into the design of her own artwork. For example, CoCo reviewed *Father's Chinese Opera* (Lo, 2014) after reading it.

> 我给这本书 5 stars. 因为像太极。我喜欢这个 moves. 这个 about 小男孩想成为 opera. 这本书的内容是教小男孩做这个 moves. 他能做很多 moves.
>
> [I give this book 5 stars. Because it is similar to tai chi. I liked the moves. This is about a little boy wanting to be in an opera. The content of this book is to teach a little boy to practice these moves. He can make many moves.]

Her book review, as a reading product, demonstrates her understanding of the book, her connections to it, and her evaluation of this book.

Knowing the routine of the book club, CoCo actively planned for her projects in our discussions. She shared that *Amy Wu and the Patchwork Dragon* (Zhang, 2020) "give (gave) me a lot of idea(s)."

> 我想要做一个 dragon. A different idea. I want to make an eastern dragon. 中国龙大概长这个样子。我一看这个，觉得很熟悉这个龙。就觉得很熟悉，没有见过。西方龙是这个样子（书里）。
>
> [I want to make one dragon. A different idea. I want to make an eastern dragon. The Chinese dragon probably looks like this. When I saw this, I felt very familiar with this dragon. I thought it was very familiar, and I had never seen it. A Western dragon is like this (in the book).]

Similarly to this response, CoCo brainstormed her drawing ideas after reading *I Dream of Popo* (Blackburne, 2021). She mentioned dreaming of lǎolao—grandmother on mom's side, seeing lǎolao in China, and video-chatting with lǎolao. Her response extended from discussing her connections, wonders, and confusions and learning cultural heritage to reviewing books and designing her artifacts.

Creating Multimodal Artifacts

CoCo demonstrated her understanding of the books and developed her cultural awareness and mixed identities through designing and creating multimodal products. She integrated her knowledge of Chinese heritage culture, American culture, and transnational experience.

Imitating Mentor Texts

CoCo used picturebooks as mentor texts and imitated their illustrations. For instance, she wrote and illustrated her four-page book, "The Big Mooncake," of a little girl and a big mooncake dedicated to Ling after reading *The Big Mooncake for Little Star* (Lin, 2018). After reading *My Day with Gong Gong* (Yee, 2020) and noticing Chinatown in the illustrations, CoCo drew a picture of Chinatown in Atlanta, which she had visited previously (see Figure 4.1). CoCo's drawing resembled the illustration of the gate in the book, with pedestrian crossing lines. Additionally, one page in the book depicts a scene of a girl and her grandfather walking across the street. Therefore, CoCo created a similar visual presentation of her crossing the street with her grandfather in Chinatown. Above the Chinatown gate in her picture, CoCo designed a red flag with a yellow star, symbolizing China's national flag. CoCo switched between Chinese and English when she described her drawing and added the text in English, "Chinatown" and a warning sign "for cars, waiting: wach [watch] out for cars." CoCo described, "这是我画的 Chinatown。这是我和外公。然后这是斑马线。[This is my drawing of Chinatown. This is my grandfather and me. This is zebra lines—a crosswalk.] 上面是 [Up here is] waiting, watch out for cars." Her language choice and illustration indicated CoCo's bilingual and bicultural identities.

In a later session, we read *Feast of Treats for the High Summer Days* (Bao, 2010), which features a little girl and her grandma walking through street markets and temple fairs for traditional snacks and performances in Beijing. CoCo borrowed Bao's book (2010) as her mentor text and designed a similar story detailing a day of her and her grandmother's shopping in China (Figure 4.2). CoCo depicted this story based on her own lived experience and titled it "My

China Adventure with Grandma." Different from Bao's picturebook (2010) that we read, CoCo redesigned hers into a ten-scene comic featuring two main characters, CoCo and her grandmother (lǎolao), in three different locations: home, restaurant, and store. She attempted to draw China's national flag on each building. Additionally, she designed speech bubbles in the panel. Under the title, her grandma said, "I'm so excited to show you China!" and CoCo responded, "I'm excited, too!" The story and the conversation reflect CoCo's appreciation of her cultural heritage and identity.

FIGURE 4.1 Picture of Chinatown

FIGURE 4.2 My China Adventure with Grandma

Designing Artifacts

CoCo borrowed multiple cultural artifacts mentioned in the picturebooks and designed her own using various material resources at home, which supported her bilingual and bicultural development. For example, after reading about Chinese New Year, she created fortune decorations, red couplets, a lantern, and paper dumplings. After learning about the vernal equinox—the first day of spring, she colored an egg and made green tea leaves.

Name Stamp. I shared our family stamps after reading *Grandfather's Stamp* (Hei, 2020), as in the findings section above. Then, CoCo decided to make a Chinese name stamp. She designed a measurement blueprint and its composition (Figure 4.3).

CoCo designed the length, width, and height of her stamp. She noticed the mini lion sculpture on the top of my jade stamp (many formal stamps are made with dragons or lions symbolizing power and auspiciousness). She then decided to choose a horse for hers because she was born in the year of the horse, following the Chinese zodiac. CoCo wrote her Chinese name on the stamp and sketched a horse on its top. Subsequently, I asked her about the stamp shape and encouraged her to create a three-dimensional blueprint. Afterward, CoCo

FIGURE 4.3 Name Stamp Design

redesigned her stamp with more details. Following that, CoCo shared her plans, and we discussed the materials for the stamp.

CoCo: I can't use these sticks (to make a name stamp). They won't roll well.
Yang: 对的，那你觉得呢？ [Right, what do you think (you can use to make a name stamp)?]
CoCo: I can collect the large stones.
Yang: 你也可以 [You can also] draw on playdough.
CoCo: 但是它是不会 save 的。[But it won't save.] I want to save my work.
Yang: 那用… [Then use…]

CoCo: Wood?

Yang: 哦。用木头你怎么刻啊？木头稍微难了一些。你现在的手太小。如果用锥子刻，很容易伤到手。胡萝卜也挺的不久。 [Oh. How do you carve it out of wood? Wood is a little hard. Your hands are too small now. If you use an awl to carve, it is easy to hurt your hands. Carrots also can't stay long.]

CoCo: 胡萝卜是吃的。[Carrots are for eating.] They would be gross.

Yang: 也可以刻的。 [They can be carved.]

CoCo: 我决定了。 [I decided.]

Yang: 但是你想要留的久就不行。我们目前的材料没有办法能让你把它长久留下的。你用 playdough 也行，然后你就让它干在那儿了，它就硬了。就变硬了，是不是？咱们就不放盒里，让它变硬，就像你以前做的那些。 [But you can't make it stay long. There is no way for you to keep it for a long time with our current materials. You can also use playdough, and then you let it dry there, and it will become hard. It becomes hard, right? Let's just leave it in the box and let it harden, like the ones you made before.]

CoCo: 嗯。 [Okay.]

CoCo and I considered available found objects when selecting materials, including playdough, wood, and carrots. I suggested several options for CoCo as she created and designed her name stamp. This multimodal artwork progressed from reading the book and visualizing her name stamp to a blueprint of size and composition and then to a playdough name stamp. Through creating a Chinese name stamp, CoCo continued to develop her heritage cultural identity.

Self-Portrait. CoCo extended the book content with her own cultural understanding, experiences, and thoughts. After reading *Watercress* (Wang, 2021), she sketched a pull-out self-portrait with a pencil. The picture shows a figure of a girl when it is folded from the middle. When it is unfolded, the body part releases a family photo collage of picking and eating a wild edible plant. This pull-out self-portrait allows her to tell her family stories.

Watercolor and Poem. After reading *Morning Market in Lotus Town* (Zhou, 2018)—a story of a child's visit to the morning market in a southern watertown where many of the streets are canals of water, CoCo drew a watercolor picture of a southern town in China with small townhouses in the background and lily pads and a water lily in the center. Also, in this picture frame, CoCo borrowed a sentence from an ancient Chinese poem about waterlilies and copied the sentence in Chinese on her picture. Then, she signed her name with a pen and stamped her name in traditional Chinese characters with her name chop in red ink. She also dated with Chinese characters, borrowing the traditional Chinese calendar. Traditional Chinese paintings often integrate painting, calligraphy, stamp signature, and date. CoCo's artwork shows a strong sense of her cultural heritage and language understanding (Figure 4.4).

FIGURE 4.4 Waterlily and Watertown

CoCo's picture after reading *Grandmother's Green Rice Balls* (Bao, 2021b) included the mixed festival celebrations of Qingming, a tomb-sweeping day in early spring from China, and Easter from the United States, which are around the same time of year. She drew flowers, kites, and colorful Easter eggs in one picture. Then she wrote an ancient Chinese poem about Qingming and wrote "Happy eastr [Easter]!!!!!!" at the bottom. Her product shows her understanding of mixed customs from both cultures.

Transnational Story. In addition to her bicultural identities in the United States setting, CoCo made transnational connections (Compton-Lilly et al., 2019) in her artwork, where she illustrated her lived-through experiences in China and the United States, along with her bilingual development (Figures 4.2 and 4.5). When analyzing the contents and cultural aspects of the artworks, for example, after reading *I Dream of Popo* (Blackburne, 2021), CoCo drew a picture of different things she did with her lǎolao in China and in the United States (Figure 4.5). She depicted her transnational experience of traveling to China and living in the United States with her parents and grandmother. In her paintings, she placed stars next to the names of the two countries. CoCo connected to the flags of these two countries in her responses. Analyzing the cultural aspects, CoCo chose red to draw things that she did in China and blue to draw things that she did in the United States. Red is commonly used to represent China and Chinese culture. The content of her drawing also shows her cultural competence (Ladson-Billings, 2021). CoCo recognized her home culture of making and eating dumplings and wearing qipao—a Chinese dress, as she created this artwork. This drawing reveals her multiple identities as a Chinese American girl.

FIGURE 4.5 Me with “外婆” (Lǎolao) in U.S.A. and China

CoCo described her picture to the group in the reading club, “在 China 里边我们正在吃饺子，做的饺子。我们正在一个大 table 上吃。我非常喜欢吃饺子。[In the China part, we are eating dumplings, homemade dumplings. We are eating at a big table. I like eating dumplings very much.]” She continued to explain the clothes, “我在中国的时候我画我和姥姥和你，都穿的是旗袍。[When I was in China, I painted lǎolao, you (mom), and me, wearing qipao (a traditional Chinese dress).]” CoCo’s drawing and verbal description reflected her bilingual and bicultural identity.

The examples above show that CoCo used a mix of modes to respond to the picturebooks and design her artifacts. She constantly used texts and images for her products, adopting different materials: pencils, crayons, colored pencils, colored markers, watercolor, playdough, magazines, toothpicks, bowls, and her name stamp. CoCo created a variety of genres and artifacts as her reading responses and presented her cultural and language identities in her artifacts.

Developing Languages

CoCo actively engaged with her full linguistic repertoire while discussing culturally relevant picture books with other families of similar linguistic and cultural backgrounds. She seamlessly switched between Chinese and English as she expressed her thoughts, discussed her questions, and made connections during discussions and in her creative artifacts.

The goal of this community-based book club was to support Chinese American children in learning their heritage culture and language. As a result, the workshop was conducted in both English and Mandarin Chinese. Although CoCo used both languages during the discussions, her dominant language remained Chinese. For example, we primarily spoke in Chinese in the above conversation about designing a name stamp. However, when the book was in English only, CoCo incorporated English keywords from the text into her speech. When she struggled to express herself in Chinese, CoCo adjusted her wording or rephrased her thoughts for communication. At times, she translated into English or borrowed English words to clarify her understanding of Chinese texts.

In her creative work, CoCo incorporated print texts into 23 out of the 28 artifacts she designed. She created six artifacts entirely in Chinese and eight solely in English, including a card, a life cycle, a kite, a Chinatown-themed piece, a garden activity book, a Mid-Autumn Festival booklet, and a comic. After reading *The Ugly Vegetables* (Lin, 2001), she designed an eight-page activity book titled "The Garden Activities for Children of All Ages" in English. This book featured seven interactive activities, including math problems, answering questions, fill-in-the-blank about the reader's personal connections, a drawing prompt for a garden, and tracing activities for word practice. This demonstrates how CoCo actively connected reading to her learning experiences and thought about using interactive activities for reading engagement.

Similarly, after reading and talking about *Thanking the Moon: Celebrating the Mid-Autumn Festival* (Lin, 2010), CoCo wrote a three-chapter book in English titled "Mid-Autumn Festival." Each chapter contained a title, text, and an illustration. Her book products highlight her ability to engage with multiple genres and transition from a reader to an author. Furthermore, they reflect the influence of English as her instructional language at school and her access to predominantly English-language texts.

CoCo also produced nine bilingual products, with almost equivalent input in both languages. For example, after reading *Red Is a Dragon: A Book of Colors* (Thong, 2008), she designed a bilingual book, "CoCo 的色彩书 [CoCo's Color Book]." Each of the seven pages featured one of the seven rainbow colors. For each color, she chose a piece of construction paper of that matching color as the background and wrote the objects representing that color in two languages. She described the colorful objects from her surroundings and her culture. Then, she cut out an object representing that color from a magazine and glued it on that page. For example, the original book contains the following lines:

> Red is a dragon
> Red is a drum
> Red are the firecrackers – here they come.
>
> (Thong, 2008, p. 2)

FIGURE 4.6 The Red Color Page from CoCo's Bilingual Color Book [Translation of the Chinese text: Red is dancing dragon, rose flower, (and) watermelon.]

CoCo borrowed the original sentence structure for her English text, while her Chinese sentence followed a similar pattern. She translated "dragon" to 舞龙 [dancing dragon], "rose" to 玫瑰花 [rose flower], and "watermelon in my hand" to 西瓜 [watermelon]. Although she did not translate word-for-word, her selected Chinese words better expressed the meaning. She wrote on red construction paper, cut an image of watermelon slices from a magazine, and glued it onto the paper.

After drawing Figure 4.5, CoCo described how she helped her lǎolao understand an English signboard when they visited a zoo in the United States. CoCo utilized translanguaging in her writing to describe her experience. She wrote both the Chinese character "马" and the English word "horse" in the speech bubbles to indicate that she used both Chinese and English in her conversation with lǎolao. She taught lǎolao the English pronunciation and its Chinese meaning. CoCo demonstrated her bilingual identity by using translanguaging in her picture and verbal descriptions of her picture.

Overall, CoCo leveraged her linguistic repertoire to discuss the books and create her multimodal artifacts, which in turn supported her bilingual development. Her language use in the discussion and creative artifacts reflects her bilingual identity as a Chinese American. One key finding from her responses is that CoCo's strong sense of agency stood out in her learning process as an author and an artist. She took ownership of her learning beyond the book club. The reasons could be that she felt comfortable in this virtual community with peers who shared similar linguistic and cultural backgrounds and a parent and a teacher who knew her better and provided scaffolding. Her extensive exposure to multicultural and international books, combined with deep connections to her cultural heritage, enriched her knowledge and confidence. Through consistent journaling and creative projects, CoCo developed into a self-assured writer who actively shaped her own learning experiences.

Discussion

CoCo developed bicultural identities through reading culturally relevant picturebooks, engaging in cultural discussions at home, sharing experiences with other families of similar cultural backgrounds, creating multimodal products, and employing translanguaging practices throughout. Those findings contribute to a better understanding of young children's bilingual and bicultural development when centering their conversations with their parents about culturally relevant literature books and multimodal responses to picturebooks.

Picturebooks as Sliding Glass Doors

The picturebooks discussed in this chapter serve as windows for CoCo to learn about her cultural heritage, mirrors to see her cultural connections, and sliding glass doors to see her mixed identities (Bishop, 1990). She identified the main characters as Asian Americans by noticing their skin color and appearance. However, CoCo and many other Asian American children were not born with an inherent understanding of their cultural heritage. Instead, they negotiated their cultures and identities through lived experiences (Hao, 2023). Their home contexts and ethnic communities in the United States and their relationships with their relatives overseas are their ways of connecting to their roots. Reading literature books and conferring with parents and other families with similar backgrounds helped CoCo develop her cultural awareness and build her identity.

Many contemporary Chinese American picturebooks feature transgenerational relationships between the main characters and their grandparents (Wang et al., 2022), a theme reflected in the picturebooks selected in the workshop. This theme resonated with CoCo's real-life experiences, as her grandparents lived in Mainland China. She frequently referenced her relationship with her lǎolao and other relatives when discussing her connections to China and Chinese culture. Her awareness of her cultural heritage was reinforced through these transgenerational relationships. Reading and discussing the selected picturebooks further encouraged transnational awareness, sparking her interest in visiting China, exploring new places in China, and learning more about Chinese traditions and festival customs. Such transgenerational relationships helped CoCo and other second-generation immigrant children build transnational connections.

Family Effort for Identity Building

Literacy development occurs within a network of experiences at home and within larger communities (Kim & Song, 2019). When the home environment differs from a child's broader community, they may experience confusion regarding identifying cultural identity. In such cases, assimilation and generalization may not suffice in fostering an understanding of cultural heritage and identities. Open discussions about these differences and uncertainties are crucial for young children. In this chapter, CoCo developed her bilingual and bicultural identities by discussing her questions and cultural connections at home and with other Chinese American families in the book club. As her parent, I shared more cultural traditions related to the picturebooks as well as regional differences in food and customs. I helped her compare the differences between Chinese and American holidays and clarified her misconceptions. Hearing about cultural variations and differences through books, family discussions, and group conversations helped CoCo negotiate her understanding of cultures and identities, ultimately fostering a sense of belonging to her ethnic group.

A child is not born with a language or cultural heritage but develops cultural awareness through lived experiences. CoCo recognized that cultural knowledge is not solely dependent on language proficiency. For example, she noted that some authors of Chinese American books did not speak Chinese. Children acquire their knowledge from the environment and make inferences from their ever-growing funds of knowledge (Moll et al., 1992), which may sometimes be limited or mixed with ambiguous cultural information they are unaware of. Many first-generation immigrants perceive a distinct boundary between American and Chinese cultures. However, for the second-generation children growing up in immigrant families in the United States, this boundary is less defined, and their cultural identity is a fusion of Eastern and Western influences. For instance, CoCo labeled American food as Chinese (e.g., waffles) because she ate them at home. She mistakenly believed that Chinatown was in China based on its name and created a blend of Eastern and Western cultural celebrations. These findings suggest that family conversations about such topics are essential in helping children negotiate and shape their cultural identities.

Multimodality for Multiple Identities

Family members enhance children's literacy development by integrating diverse and enriching literacy activities into their daily lives (Taylor, 1983). This chapter illustrates a Chinese American family's rich and multimodal home literacy environment in a suburban area of the southeastern United States. CoCo had access to various material resources at home, including books, colored pencils, markers, paint, playdough, construction paper, and stamps. These plentiful material resources enabled her to express her meaning-making of the picturebooks, take ownership of various creative artifacts, develop her cultural awareness, and reflect on her bicultural identities in the family book club. She constructed her identities by reading books, discussing them with her parents, creating artifacts, and sharing her work with peers who shared similar backgrounds.

Books served as mentor texts for her artistic creations. CoCo designed and redesigned products to represent herself (Janks et al., 2013). Her multiple layers of reading response were akin to peeling an onion—she made connections, posed questions, and formulated her own interpretations (Hao, 2023). Initially, she imitated objects from the books, but over time, she began designing her own original artifacts. Her multimodal responses indicated deeper levels of thinking after reading and discussing the books. The discussion and multimodal creation provide reciprocal processes for her to maintain her cultural identity, develop new identities, and gain confidence in her evolving identities.

Language as the Goal, the Tool, and Identity

CoCo employed her full linguistic repertoire while responding to the culturally relevant picturebooks. She demonstrated her translanguaging practices while discussing books, drawing, writing, and creating artifacts. CoCo engaged in translanguaging practices during their multimodal product creation. These findings align with previous studies showing that translanguaging practices support bilingual children's reading comprehension and development (Moody et al., 2021; Yang et al., 2021).

One objective of this book club was for children to learn their heritage language. Therefore, bilingual books and read-aloud activities were implemented. However, only one-third of the books were bilingual, highlighting the limited availability of high-quality bilingual picturebooks. Like other Chinese American children in this family project, CoCo primarily used English at school and Chinese at home. Translanguaging was an integral part of her meaning-making process. CoCo viewed language as both a tool for cultural exploration and an essential aspect of a person's cultural identity. Although all of the picturebooks introduced Chinese culture, none addressed critical or controversial topics related to race or equity. Including books that explore these themes could help children gain a deeper understanding of social justice issues and develop advocacy skills.

Implications

These findings have implications for future research and practices aimed at involving parents and fostering community engagement to support bilingual children's identity development. Findings from long-term studies enhance our understanding of bilingual children's home literacy practices. This research employed an ethnographic case study of a bilingual family in a virtual book club. Further research could examine the impact of bilingual families on children's linguistic and cultural identities, bicultural families' responses to culturally relevant literature books, and bilingual children's designing and redesigning of multimodal artifacts as a form of their identity representations.

Literacy and language teachers and researchers should communicate and collaborate with parents – virtually and in person – to foster young children's bilingual and bicultural development at home. For example, bilingual parents can be advised about what types of multicultural and international literature books they can read with their children, what kinds of materials they can prepare for their children at home, what resources they can find to support their children's bilingual development, and how to confer with their children about literature books and their bicultural identities. Teachers, parents, and children could work together to extend the children's cultural knowledge (Hao, 2024).

When working with bilingual families and communities, language teachers and researchers should encourage their use of full linguistic resources to make meaning. For instance, in a community or family book club, teachers can allow time for the family to lead the book talk (Moody et al., 2021). Teachers can select culturally relevant picturebooks that reflect the children's family histories and experiences to help families reflect on their identities and support their children's use of their full linguistic repertoires.

Language teachers can assist parents who are raising bilingual children to understand the importance of providing a rich multimodal home literacy environment. Teachers can develop a handout for parents that includes a list of free or inexpensive recommended materials and examples of artwork. Teachers can talk to the school or local librarians about creating a text set of heritage books and suggest ideas for families to read and talk about books within their families or with other families in their community. Teachers can also provide parents with suggestions on how to utilize their home material resources to support their children's biliteracy development at home. By fostering strong partnerships between educators and parents, children can receive meaningful support in developing their bilingual and bicultural identities.

Inquiry Questions

Questions for Researchers:

- How do bilingual children maintain their heritage languages and cultures?
- How do bilingual children build their linguistic and cultural identities through reading and responding to culturally relevant literature?

- What can families do to support young children's heritage language learning and linguistic and cultural identity development?

Questions for Teachers:

- How can teachers select culturally relevant children's literature books for bilingual students?
- How can teachers scaffold bilingual students' reading responses to culturally relevant books?
- How can teachers leverage students' linguistic repertoires to develop their literacy skills?

Questions for Parents:

- How can parents effectively read and discuss picturebooks with young children?
- What strategies can parents use to support children's biliteracy development at home?
- What community resources are available to help children learn their heritage language?

Suggested Reading

Brown, S., & Hao, L. (Eds.). (2022). *Multimodal literacies in young emergent bilinguals: Beyond print-centric practices* (Vol. 105). Channel View.

Brown, S., & Zhang, R. (2024). *Multimodal funds of knowledge in literacy: Countering deficit narratives of diverse families*. Taylor & Francis.

Chen, X., & Browne, S. (2023). *Multicultural books for preK–grade three: A guide for classroom teachers*. Rowman & Littlefield.

Rodríguez, N. N., An, S., & Kim, E. J. (2023). *Teaching Asian America in elementary classrooms*. Routledge.

5

"好! FINE! ¡PERFECTO!"

Journey to Becoming Trilingual

Globalization has expanded opportunities and increased demands for multilingual learners. Approximately 43% of the world's population is bilingual, with around 17% being multilingual who speak three or more languages or dialects (Gration, 2023). In the United States, approximately 21.6% of the population is bilingual, with 13.4% speaking Spanish and 3.5% speaking Asian and Pacific Islander languages, according to the U.S. Census Bureau (n.d.). Spanish is the most popular additional language to learn, followed by Japanese, Korean, French, and Chinese in the United States (Gration, 2023).

Much research has explored English-Spanish bilingualism (Daniel & Pacheco, 2016; García, 2020; García & Schleppegrell, 2021; Salmerón, 2022) and English-Chinese bilingualism (Yang et al., 2021; Zheng, 2021) in the United States context. Each language requires different language maintenance strategies, and a trilingual child may develop a richer and more differentiated language and cultural awareness than monolingual and bilingual children (Braun & Cline, 2014). However, few studies examine trilingualism involving English, Spanish, and Chinese. Becoming trilingual can facilitate children's cultural and political exchanges, promote their understanding and appreciation of diverse cultures, enrich their lives, create more cultural, linguistic, academic, and social opportunities, and even boost their brainpower (Wang, 2008). This chapter presents the experiences of CoCo, a Chinese-English bilingual child learning Spanish through reading Spanish children's literature books when she was seven years old. This chapter explores the following research questions:

- How does a Chinese-English bilingual child read and respond to Spanish picturebooks?

DOI: 10.4324/9781003517061-5

- How does the child use her full linguistic repertoire to learn a third language?

Context

In the state where this study was conducted, 91.46% of the residents were monolingual English speakers. The largest non-English speaking group was Latinx, comprising 3.76% of the population. Asian or Pacific Islanders comprised about 2.84% of the state population (Columbia Population, 2023). While the state had several Mandarin Chinese two-way immersion programs and Spanish two-way immersion programs, CoCo's school district only offered a world language program but did not hold any dual-language immersion programs. Within the world language program, Spanish was the most widely offered foreign language from elementary through high school, and several other foreign languages, such as French, German, Chinese, and Latin, were offered at a few different schools. The vast majority of students learned Spanish as their foreign language, as it was so prevalent.

CoCo's exposure to Spanish began in one of her first-grade related art classes, and she has had weekly Spanish language lessons since then. The first-grade Spanish teacher displayed a strong interactive teaching style, even in a virtual synchronous classroom. The teacher's screen depicted a beautiful portrait of her sitting in front of the monitor, with a big colorful flower in her hair. She knew ventriloquism and taught with her assistant Ali, an alligator puppet. When the teacher showed her slides, she even changed her cursor into a smiley face. The teacher enthusiastically welcomed students into her virtual class with a big smile across her face. For all 40 minutes of her Spanish lesson, the children were highly motivated to participate in the conversations and say Spanish words and sentences after their teacher and her assistant, Ali. Her class was always full of laughter. I was attracted to her dynamic teaching style. For this reason, I occasionally sat next to CoCo during Spanish class and learned Spanish alongside her. After class, CoCo and I used Mango (n.d.)—a language learning website that we could access for free via the local public library system at that time and checked out Spanish and bilingual (English and Spanish) picturebooks from that library.

CoCo wanted to learn Spanish and had a strong interest and motivation, as she shared in an interview,

> 我觉得非常好，因为我不学我就不能去西班牙语的地方。有人问我，是一个很好的交流 chance。
> [I think it's very good, because if I don't learn it, I can't go to a place where Spanish is spoken. (If) someone asks me (in Spanish), it's a good chance to communicate.]

Additionally, CoCo shared that she knew some people who spoke German, Japanese, and Spanish. Therefore, her enthusiasm extended to aspirations of learning French and German in the future. CoCo expressed that she wanted to shop first before she chose one language to study further,

> 每个都学一点点。最后我再看学哪个。我会根据我想要突破的东西，在我眼前。因为我可以跟更多的人一起说话。
>
> [Learn a little bit of each (language). And then, I will decide which one to learn. I'll (decide) based on what I want to break through, right in front of my eyes. Because I can talk to more people.]

CoCo was eager to use Spanish to communicate with more different people. Subsequently, she included learning Spanish in her self-portrait as part of her identity, as shown in Figure 1.2. On the left leg in the self-portrait, she wrote, "learning Spanish, Espanile [Español]." CoCo said,

> 因为可以突破我的记录，可以让我开心。我想突破一个单词，或者书， 一直到我可以跟别人说话。跟别人不同，因为我会三种语言。
>
> [Because (I) can break my record, (and it) makes me happy. I want to learn a word or (read a) book until I can talk to other people. I'm different from others because I'm trilingual.]

Reading Spanish Literature Books

Reading is a transaction between the reader, text, and context; readers make connections with the reading text and create their own meanings (Rosenblatt, 2005a). Readers learn language, learn about language, and learn through language by reading (Halliday, 1982; Mills & Stephens, 2004). Given CoCo's dual interest in learning Spanish and children's literature, she and I selected books together and invited a tutor to read with us each week when CoCo was a second grader (seven years and four months old). The tutor was a junior doctoral student who spoke Chinese, Korean, English, and Spanish. She studied Spanish literature in her undergraduate and master's programs. We met weekly for 45 minutes each time and for a total of six meetings over two months. Due to the COVID pandemic, five meetings were held via video conferencing, and one was in person.

CoCo selected picturebooks in Spanish from those books that we checked out from the local public library and our home collection. Table 5.1 lists the selected books following the order of the sessions. All books were either printed in Spanish only or in both Spanish and English.

At the end of each session, CoCo was invited to write or draw what she had learned from the session. Each session was audio recorded and transcribed. I took observation notes and collected all of CoCo's work samples. Data were

TABLE 5.1 Selected Spanish Books

Session #	*Text Selection*	*Author*	*Illustrator*	*Publication Year*	*Language(s)*
1	*Dormiré La Siesta! [I will Take a Nap.]*	Mo Willems	Mo Willems	2021	Spanish
2	*My Colors, My World / Mis Colores, Mi Mundo*	Maya Christina Gonzales	Maya Christina Gonzales	2013	Spanish and English
3	Wheels on the Bus / Las Ruedas Del Camión in *Sing with me / Canta Conmigo*	Jose-Luis Orozco	Sara Palacios	2020	Spanish and English
4	The Eensy, Weensy Spider / La Araña Pequeñita in *Sing with Me / Canta Conmigo*	Jose-Luis Orozco	Sara Palacios	2020	Spanish and English
5	*¡Hoy Volare! [Today I will Fly.]*	Mo Willems	Mo Willems	2015	Spanish
6	*Estamos en un Libro [We are in a Book]*	Mo Willems	Mo Willems	2015	Spanish

open-coded, and themes emerged from the data to answer the research questions (Creswell & Creswell, 2018; Merriam, 2009; Stake, 1995). In the following sections, I will report the findings regarding CoCo's identifying similarities and differences between the three languages, purposes and functions of using different languages, and translanguaging and linguistic repertoire.

Identifying Similarities and Differences between the Three Languages

Interestingly, CoCo noticed similarities and differences between Mandarin Chinese, English, and Spanish. She reported in an interview,

> 学起来一样，因为都有自己的规律，都有自己的东西。
>
> [Learning (those three languages) is the same because they all have their own rules and their own things.]

First, CoCo identified that the sounds are different in the three languages as she explained, "不同的音，但是英文就是平音。[(They all have) different sounds, but English is flat (without intonation change).]" Correspondingly in the sessions, she learned that the accent changed the sound in Spanish, for instance, sí and si. CoCo further explained the differences and her struggle by saying,

> 我觉得西班牙语就有点难，因为那些字跟中文和英文都不一样，是另一些声音。中文有拼音，英文没有拼音。西班牙语有中国的声音，但不写出来。有上，下，但没有像中文。
>
> [I think Spanish is a bit difficult because those words are different from words in Chinese and English, and they have different sounds. Chinese has pinyin (phonetic system), but English does not have pinyin. Spanish has Chinese sounds, but they are not spelled out. There are up and down (tones), but they are not like (the tones in) Chinese.]

Second, she knew that the graphic systems were different between those three languages. She clarified as below,

> 中文的字你得写好才能称一个单词。不然差一笔就是别的字了。相似是都有自己的字，你可以读。中文有拼音A 到Z。西班牙语跟英文一样，跟中文汉字 strokes， 学起来都是一样的突破力。
>
> [A Chinese character can only be called a word if you write it well. Otherwise, it will be a different word when missing one stroke. The similarity is that each has its own word that you can read. Chinese has pinyin letters from A to Z. Spanish is like English. Chinese characters have strokes. Learning those three languages is the same. (You need to) breakthrough.]

CoCo knew the importance of accuracy in writing Chinese characters since it is a logographic language, and missing one stroke of a character would result in a change of meaning (see more about the Chinese language in Chapter 1).

Third, when she read, CoCo noticed the differences in Spanish punctuation. For instance, a question in Spanish is marked with a normal question mark at the end and an upside-down question mark at the beginning of a sentence, whereas English and Chinese only use a question mark at the end of a sentence.

Fourth, CoCo realized that the sentence structure in Spanish varied from Chinese and English. For instance, in Spanish, CoCo learned that she needed to change both nouns and adjectives into plural forms. When she learned "orange flowers [flores anaranjadas]" in Spanish in session 2, she pointed out that the order in Spanish was "flowers orange." She used Chinese to express her understanding of the order of those words by saying, "花橘色 [flower orange color]."

Yang: 橘色还有花。我们先说？我们先说什么？[Orange color and flowers. We first say? What shall we say first?]

CoCo: 花，橘色。[Flowers, orange color.]

Yang: 对，他们就是先说花。[Yes, they (Spanish speakers) say flowers first.]
CoCo: 花色橘。[Flowers color orange.]
Yang: 不能全反。但是英文也是跟中文一样的吗？[Not all characters can be reversed (in Chinese). But is English the same as Chinese?]
CoCo: 嗯。[Yes.]
Yang: 英文跟中文一样，但是 Spanish 就不一样了。[English is the same as Chinese, but Spanish is different.]
CoCo: 嗯。[Yes.]

Overall, CoCo was interested in learning the Spanish language and had confidence in learning, even though she realized the differences between those three languages. She said,

> 还可以，因为我总是练习，所以我会越来越好。有点难，发音不相似。很简单，那些音学会有人指导，就会更突破，更有信心。
>
> [It's okay because I'm always practicing, so I'm getting better and better. (Learning Spanish) is kind of hard, (because) the pronunciation is not similar. It would be very easy if someone could guide me to learn the sound. Then I will break through more and be more confident.]

CoCo furthermore identified areas that she needed to improve. The quote above also indicates her confidence and agency in learning Spanish.

Purposes and Functions of Using Different Languages

The overall analysis showed that CoCo had different purposes using the three languages. Table 5.2 presents CoCo's language use during the reading sessions, followed by descriptions of each category. As can be seen from Table 5.2, Chinese was the functional language that CoCo used for communication, English was the content language she relied on to understand the text, and Spanish was the target language that she was learning. The codes identified in her responses indicate that CoCo used the Chinese language for pragmatic purposes and English and Spanish language for mathetic purposes—learning purposes (Halliday, 1982).

Use of Chinese

CoCo only spoke Chinese when the tutor and I spoke Chinese to her. When the tutor talked in English, she seldom switched to Chinese in her talk. CoCo used Chinese mainly for the purposes of clarifying the questions and confirming her answers; asking about the Spanish word pronunciation, word meaning, word differences, text meaning, and special marks, e.g., "Puedo 是什么意思啊？ [What is the meaning of Puedo?]" (Session 6); answering questions and

TABLE 5.2 CoCo's Language Use

Use of Chinese	*Use of English*	*Use of Spanish*
• Notice text features • Clarify questions and confirm answers • Ask about the Spanish word pronunciation, word meaning, word differences, text meaning, and special marks • Answer questions from the tutor and the parent, and guess word's meaning • Identify language differences within Spanish • Translate into Chinese to show her understanding of the grammar rules in Spanish • Connect to prior knowledge • Express her opinion, knowing, or not knowing • Share her work and invite others to share	• Keep the authors' names and places in English • Look at the English version when meeting the unknown Spanish words • Ask to clarify and for Spanish expressions and text meaning • Check if she is right • Answer questions • Give the translation of Spanish words • Guess or give the sentence meaning and word's meaning from Spanish and Chinese • Share her inference and express understanding • Use picture clues • Express her uncertainty, difficulty, unknown things, struggle, and feeling • Evaluate the texts • Logistics: agenda, notetaking • Share and sing	• Read-aloud texts • Repeat the texts • Give translated words for English or Chinese words • Pronunciation and sound • Closure in one session

guessing the word meaning; connecting to her prior knowledge, e.g., "我们学过在那个网上 [We learned that before from the internet]" (Session 5); expressing her opinion, what she knows and what she does not know; and sharing her work and inviting others to do the same. For example, CoCo asked to share her map of Spanish-speaking countries in the world that she drew in Figure 5.1. She relied on the Chinese language to talk about her work and borrowed English words when she mentioned many countries and places.

CoCo: 你看我做的这个。[Look at what I did.]
Yang: We can talk about it.
Tutor: Umhum.
Yang: 你讲一下。妈妈拍了照片了，但是还没来得及上传。我来帮你hold吧。你来讲。[You talk about it. Mom took a picture but had no time to upload it yet. Let me help you hold (it). You talk about (it).]

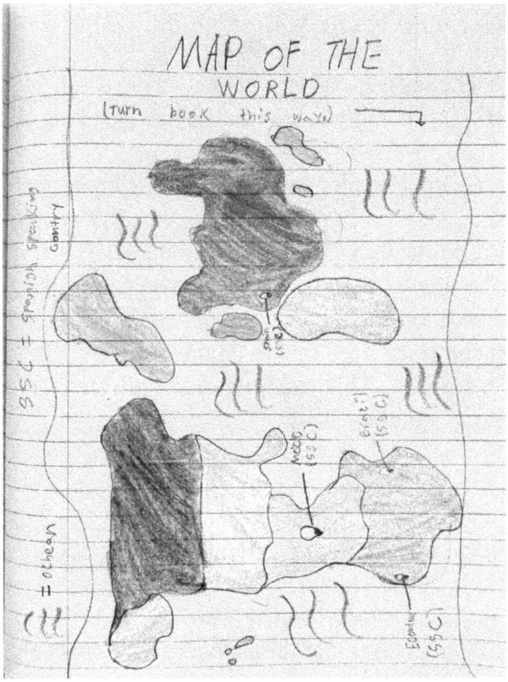

FIGURE 5.1 CoCo's Map of the World

CoCo: 这个是我们住的地方。这是 Hawaii。这是 Alaska。这是 Canada。这是那个 Mexico。然后我写的SSC是这，Spanish-speaking country。这个小的 wave 是 ocean。这个地方是中国。这是，这个地方大概是日本。这个是 Africa。这是那种的，哎呦，是叫什么来的呀，哎呦，那个，J— 你听不懂— [This is where we live. This is Hawaii. This is Alaska. This is Canada. This is Mexico. Then the SSC I wrote is this, Spanish-speaking country. This small wave is the ocean. This place is China. This is, this place is probably Japan. This is Africa. This is that kind of, whoops, what is it called, whoops, that, J— you don't understand—]

Yang: 这个上面是哪里? [Where is this one on the top?]

CoCo: 这是 Spain。那是 Asia。[This is Spain. That is Asia.]

Yang: 这是 Asia 啊?整个都是 Asia 吗?上次你不是这样告诉我的啊。[Is this Asia? Is it all Asia? That's not what you told me last time.]

CoCo: 这个是 — [This is —]

Yang: 噢！[Oh!]

CoCo: 然后这个是台湾。这是那个Japan。[Then this is Taiwan. This is Japan.]

Yang: Japan.

CoCo: 这个地方是 Brazil 和这个 Ecuador。 [This is Brazil, and this is Ecuador.]
Tutor: Ecuador <Laugh>.
Yang: 那你标注的 [Then you marked] Spanish-speaking countries. What are they?
CoCo: Mexico, Spain, Ecuador, and Brazil. (Session 4)

In her sharing, CoCo relied on Chinese to communicate and show the countries on the map that she drew. When it came to the names of the Spanish-speaking countries, she referred to those countries and marked them in English. The reason could be that she completed this assignment in English and learned about those countries in English. This example also indicates CoCo's identity as a trilingual speaker and a global citizen.

Use of English

The English language was the dominant language that CoCo adopted during the tutoring sessions, which was shown in her work samples and conversations. The reason could be that her school language was English, she read more texts in English, and the bilingual texts that I found were in Spanish and English. Unfortunately, I did not find any Chinese Spanish bilingual books that she could read. I located one trilingual book; however, the Spanish in that book was too challenging for CoCo to read; thus, it was not included in the book selection.

Similar to her use of Chinese, CoCo adopted English to clarify the questions, check if she understood right, answer questions, give the translation of Spanish words, guess the word and sentence meanings, and to express her uncertainty, unknown things, difficulty, struggle, and feelings (see codes in Table 5.2). For example, CoCo was uncertain about a Spanish word spelling in Session 4 and said, "I'm not sure how to spell it. Maybe I should leave (it) off here. It looks weird now." Later in the same session, when CoCo couldn't remember the meaning of a sentence, she said, "I don't know. I forgot again." Then, she also expressed her willingness to understand from the context of the texts by saying, "I will try!" Additionally, CoCo kept the authors' names, characters' names, and names of places in English even though she transferred between three languages. When she did not know any Spanish words, CoCo referred to the English version of the texts to understand.

In general, English was the medium that CoCo applied to convey the meaning. She shared her inferences and expressed her understanding in English. She also translated the Spanish text into English and explained the Spanish text in English to show her comprehension. For instance, when the tutor gave CoCo a hint about the context of using "Qué duermas bien," CoCo said, "Have good dreams." Additionally, CoCo even used English to monitor her meaning-making process. For example, she thought aloud, "mañana 我 [I] guess, you are not gonna fly in the morning, and it does not make sense" in Session 5. After reading *My Colors My World* (Gonzalez, 2013), CoCo made a vocabulary list of colors in Spanish and their English translations and used colors to indicate the words' meanings in Figure 5.2. In another session, CoCo was asked to make a world map showing Spanish-speaking countries (see Figure 5.1). She made the labels and marked the countries in English. Her work samples not only show her language usage but also indicate her adoption of multiple modes in her reading responses.

Moreover, when CoCo talked about using the clues from the illustrations in the picturebooks, she employed English. For example, in Session 5, she looked at the pictures and even pointed out the differences in the pictures for others. I asked, "Why do you say that? 你怎么发现的？[How did you find out?]" CoCo said, "Because I see his feelings. Looks hungry." When we continued reading, she called our attention and asked, "Do you notice the differences between these pictures?" Furthermore, CoCo compared the Spanish text and shared her evaluation. For instance, she commented that the text in Session 4 was "not easy (easier) for me than on the bus (text)." Lastly, CoCo used English for logistics, such as asking for the agenda, requesting that I take notes, and asking to share her work or sing for us. Her use of English shows her pragmatic purposes and agency in learning.

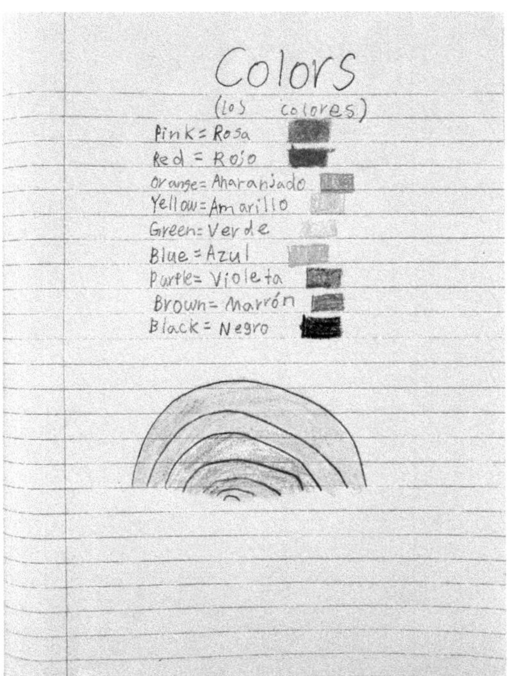

FIGURE 5.2 Colors

Use of Spanish

CoCo was a beginning Spanish learner and learned simple greetings, colors, numbers, and dates from the Spanish class at her elementary school. Her Spanish conversational proficiency was very limited at that time. During the sessions, CoCo read-aloud and repeated the texts in Spanish as the target language. She sounded out the Spanish words when she struggled. When the tutor asked for equivalent Spanish words for English or Chinese words to assess her vocabulary learning, CoCo answered in Spanish. Occasionally, CoCo used Spanish to greet the tutor at the beginning or to say bye at the end of the sessions. Moreover, she wrote in Spanish in her written responses to the texts that she read. Figure 5.3 demonstrates CoCo's notes after learning *The Wheels on the Bus* (Orozco, 2020) in Spanish. She wrote the English greetings and their Spanish translations in addition to matching pictures showing morning, noon, and evening. The finding indicates her use of Spanish for mathetic purposes, that is to say, for learning purposes (Halliday, 1982).

Translanguaging and Linguistic Repertoire

Translanguaging is the action in which bilinguals and multilinguals use their full linguistic repertoires when they read, write, speak, and listen (García &

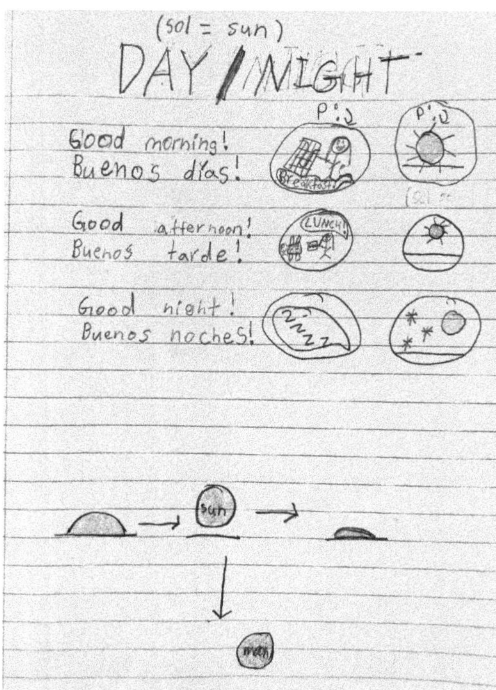

FIGURE 5.3 Day and Night Greetings

Li, 2014). Translanguaging represents a language teaching pedagogy and instruction that values learners' diverse language practices (García, 2020). Translanguaging helps bilinguals meet academic, social, and school challenges (Fu et al., 2019). CoCo, the tutor, and I applied translanguaging in our talk throughout all sessions. As a Spanish language beginner, CoCo often reads the texts in Spanish and embedded Spanish words to explain or ask about the words' meaning. She relied on English for word meaning and translation and used Chinese as the functional language to link the words within the individual sentences. When the tutor and I talked in Chinese, CoCo responded in Chinese and a mix of two or three languages. However, when we talked to her in English, her responses remained in English. The reason could be that her dominant learning language was English at school, and the monolingual view impacted her learning of other languages.

CoCo's choice of language was affected by the speaking environment and her purposes. She often mixed Chinese and English, English and Spanish; occasionally, she mixed Chinese and Spanish; she only mixed three languages to talk about word meaning, grammar patterns, or translation. She seldom repeated the same content in three languages. The only time she responded in all three languages was when she agreed to do a task, "好! Fine! ¡Perfecto!" Her translanguaging showed in the following ways: learning new words, indicating meaning in another language, transferring sound, grammar, and special marks, and mixing symbols and modes.

Learning New Words

CoCo used two to three languages in the service of learning new Spanish words. For instance, she used English for the Spanish word meaning, "mañana is tomorrow," and "Ahora ayuda is the most recent (Session 5)." And she explained her word choice in English, like "Rosa or rojo? I think it's rosa (Session 4)." Likewise, CoCo mixed English and Chinese languages to ask for the matching Spanish expression, such as, "We are flying 怎么说？ [How to say we are flying?]" or to ask for a Spanish word's meaning, including "Puedo 是什么意思啊？ [What does puedo mean?] (Session 6)" and "那这个 (próxima) 是week? [Then this (próxima) is week?] (Session 5)."

Moreover, CoCo made a new sentence in mixed codes of Spanish and English after learning the word of *gusta*, "me gusta pizza [I like pizza]." She also used mixed languages to explain the context of using a sentence, "Buenas noches 是 [is] good night! We say that when we are sleeping?" CoCo was unsure about her assumption, so she said it in a rising tone to seek for affirmance. She also mixed the languages to ask for help, like "Buenas días 怎么 spell? [How to spell good morning?] (Session 3)."

Furthermore, CoCo mixed three languages to understand word meanings. For example, "Negro [black] hair, hair怎么说? [How to say black hair?] (Session 3)." Usually, she used Spanish and English for the content words and Chinese for the functional words in this sentence pattern:

Spanish/English content words + Chinese functional words + English/Spanish content words.

For example,

"Rosa 是 [is] pink. Casas 是 [are] houses. Noche 是 [is] night? Mundo 是 [is] world." (Session 2).

"Buenas noches 是 [is] good night!" (Session 3).

"Goodbye 是 [is] adiós. Gracias por tu ayuda. 这个是 [This is] thank you for the help." (Session 5).

This sentence pattern helped her associate Spanish words with their equivalent words in English, which helped her understand the words' meanings.

Finally, CoCo efficiently chose the language to help her learn new word patterns in Spanish. For example,

CoCo: Necesito, -to, -ta [Need]?
Tutor: Who is saying this?
CoCo: Piggie. 他跟这个 elephant. 因为 elephant 是个男孩，它就是 o. [He and this elephant. Because the elephant is a boy, it should be o.] (Session 5)

This conversation indicates that CoCo was aware of the gender change in Spanish, which was different from those in English and Chinese. She also connected to her prior knowledge and gave an example of the gender difference in Spanish.

Indicating Meaning in Another Language

Since CoCo was an emergent Spanish speaker, she relied on Chinese and English to explain the meaning of the text and the differences between texts, make inferences, take notes, ask for help, share comments, and compare and contrast linguistic similarities and differences across the three languages. English was her school language and her learning language in tutoring sessions. Therefore, she relied on English for word meaning, comparing and contrasting linguistic differences between English and Spanish. Her translanguaging shows her meaning-making. For example, she explained, "Goodbye 是 [is] adiós. Gracias por tu ayuda. 这个是 [This is] thank you for the help (Session 5)" and "Great spider 然后就是 [then is] spider 就是 [is] grandotota." This example also shows her mixing three languages when she learned "The Eensy, Weensy Spider" song in Spanish.

CoCo often chose one language to explain the word's meaning and seldom explained using both languages. There was one time she explained one Spanish sentence in Chinese and the next sentence in English. "Tú no volarás hoy, 他不开心啊 [He is not happy]. 那个是 [That is], you are not gonna fly today?" (Session 5). As an emergent trilingual learner, she always used another language to convey the text's meaning.

Transferring Sound, Grammar, and Special Marks

CoCo used English phonetic knowledge to pronounce Spanish words. For example, she pronounced *me* as the English sound instead of *me* in Spanish sound. Additionally, she also mixed her syntactic knowledge across languages. She said English words in Spanish sentence order and Spanish words in English or Chinese sentence order or conventions. For example, she missed functional words in Spanish. She said "lunes mañana" instead of "mañana de lunes." Her sentence order followed English and Chinese grammar rules like "Monday morning, 星期一上午" where no functional word was being used in between. While CoCo kept learning Spanish sentence structure, she learned that adjectives followed nouns instead of the other way in English and Chinese. For instance, when she talked about the text "La araña grandotota [The great big spider]" in the song of "The Eensy, Weensy Spider," she commented,

> 这个 (grandotota) 是 great big 放在后面，然后 spider 放在前面。英文是 great big 放在前面， 然后 spider 放在后面。
> [This (grandotota) means great big, which is placed at the back, and the spider is placed at the front. In English, great big is placed in the front, and spider is placed in the back.]

This suggests that CoCo identified the syntactical differences between Spanish and English language systems, and she practiced translanguaging in her language use.

Moreover, CoCo noticed the accent mark on días and asked about it, which brought up a comparison between Spanish and Chinese phonetic systems. There is a similar rising tone mark in Chinese pinyin—the phonetic system. Dí in Spanish is pronounced with stress, which sounds like the falling tone in Chinese pinyin (dì) but looks like a rising tone in pinyin (dí). CoCo constantly mixed the Spanish accent mark and the Chinese tone mark. When she marked the fourth tone in pinyin, CoCo sometimes marked it as a Spanish accent. This transfer was also explained in Chapters 2 and 3.

Mixing Symbols and Modes

In addition to mixing languages as mentioned above, CoCo mixed different modes in her language learning process. In all the figures presented in this chapter, CoCo

FIGURE 5.4 Illustration of the Spider Song

used two languages—Spanish and English—and multiple modes. She paid attention to the text font, capitalization, layout, punctuation marks, and special marks (parentheses and equal marks). She created abbreviations, labels, and glossary boxes. Her labels in Figure 5.1 were in English only; however, her labels in the last assignment in Figure 5.4 were in Spanish and English. Figure 5.4 shows a multimodal bilingual glossary that CoCo made after learning the spider song.

Moreover, CoCo designed the pictures and used different colors and symbols to help her convey meaning. For instance, she drew the wavy line to show the ocean on the map in Figure 5.1. She made the label in English to help her readers understand her symbols and included instructions on how to read the map. In Figure 5.2, CoCo used colored pencils to draw a color mat for each color in the English–Spanish bilingual glossary and a rainbow at the bottom, including all the colors. In Figure 5.3, she drew two pictures along with each greeting sentence. The former picture indicates the activity that she did during that time, i.e., eating breakfast, eating lunch, and sleeping. The latter picture indicates the time of a day with a sun or moon. After CoCo learned *The Eensy, Weensy Spider* (Orozco, 2020), she drew a picture to illustrate this song, showing the two children, the spider, the water pipe, the rain, and the sun in Figure 5.4. CoCo labeled the objects in both English and Spanish, and she included a new word text box explaining the meaning of "big" and "small" in Spanish. Those multiple modes (Kress & van Leeuwen, 2001) and translanguaging practices facilitated her learning and represented her understanding of language use and cultural awareness.

Discussion

The reading sessions provided a meaningful space for CoCo's trilingual development and ways of knowing (García et al., 2017). This protected time and supportive learning environment nurtured CoCo's Spanish language learning. As mentioned earlier, reading is a transactional process, and readers make connections with what they read (Rosenblatt, 2005a). CoCo connected her prior knowledge and life experiences with what she was reading, which helped her construct meaning and learn a third language.

The language environment and communication needs highly impact CoCo's language use for pragmatic and mathetic purposes (Halliday, 1982). English was her school language, and it became her dominant learning language. Therefore, CoCo relied on English for the word meaning, asking questions, checking her understanding, taking notes, and sharing her work. She relied on the Chinese language to make connections. It could be that her home language was Chinese; she and I talked and discussed what she learned in Chinese, and I had reading conferences with her very often when teaching her Chinese language at home. Interestingly, when the tutoring session instruction was in Chinese, CoCo responded in both Chinese and English, yet she primarily used English to explain Spanish word meanings. When the instruction shifted to English, CoCo responded in English, and her use of Chinese diminished. Due to her emerging Spanish proficiency, CoCo engaged with Spanish predominantly through reading the text, referring to the text, and assessing her learning.

Previous research underscores that translanguaging offered various spaces for different cultures and allowed bilinguals and multilinguals to understand different cultures (García, 2020; García & Schleppegrell, 2021; Tian & Shepard-Carey, 2020). Many studies have shown that translanguaging not only allows bilinguals and multilinguals to use all their linguistic repertoires during speaking, listening, reading, and writing, but also helps learners to value various languages (Back et al., 2020; García, 2020; García & Schleppegrell, 2021; Hill et al., 2020; Kwon & Schallert, 2016; Salmerón, 2022). CoCo used her language repertoire from her own perspectives (García et al., 2017) as she compared Spanish with English and Chinese to learn the target language efficiently, transferred from one language to another, and mixed codes from two or three languages. CoCo learned Spanish as an additional language while she had already gained proficiency in English and Chinese. For this reason, she used learning strategies like making a glossary and translating the Spanish text into English to show her understanding. Translanguaging helped my emergent learner to navigate her learning of a new language using her full linguistic repertoire, reinforcing previous findings that translanguaging between different languages helped students develop their literacy skills (García, 2020; Kwon & Schallert, 2016; Rowe, 2018; Salmerón, 2022; Smith, 2020; Zheng, 2021).

Beyond different languages, multimodal literacy played a vital role in CoCo's Spanish learning process. Her self-portrait shows that she regarded herself as a proud bilingual and an emergent trilingual. Translanguaging and multimodality support forming her trilingual identities and building her cultural understanding. Prior research indicates that translanguaging contributed to shaping bilinguals' and multilinguals' academic and social identities (Back et al., 2020; Daniel & Pacheco, 2016; García, 2020; García & Schleppegrell, 2021; Yang et al., 2021). CoCo's ability to connect with texts in multiple languages highlights the importance of recognizing students' multilingual and multicultural backgrounds in language and literacy education.

Implications

The findings from this chapter underscore the need for more research on trilingual literacy development, particularly in monolingual-dominant regions where bilingual and trilingual education support is limited. Educators should cultivate translanguaging spaces that allow emergent multilingual speakers to engage with multiple languages in dynamic and meaningful ways. Rather than focusing solely on decoding the words, instruction should facilitate opportunities for multilingual children to construct and recreate meaning across languages.

Parental and community involvement is also crucial in fostering children's multilingual development. Providing children with access to more diverse linguistic resources, such as bilingual books, language-learning apps, and multilingual social opportunities, can enhance their motivation and engagement in speaking more languages. As it is important to monitor the quantity and quality of the heritage language input (Wang, 2008), it is equally important to monitor all language input in home, school, or community so that children receive consistent and meaningful interactions in all their languages. During this study, CoCo was exposed to a Spanish-speaking environment twice a week for a total of 90 minutes per week. After the session, we started using a different language learning app, Duolingo, and CoCo committed an average of 10 to 15 minutes to learning Spanish every day. Inspired by Crisfield's (2021) recommendation to track language input, I made a chart of CoCo's daily language exposure. Figure 5.5 maps her language use and commitment to learning each language so we can make learning plans accordingly. For instance, her English input was approximately eight hours, her Chinese input was four hours, and her Spanish input was 15 minutes on school days. This highlights the need for a dynamic family language

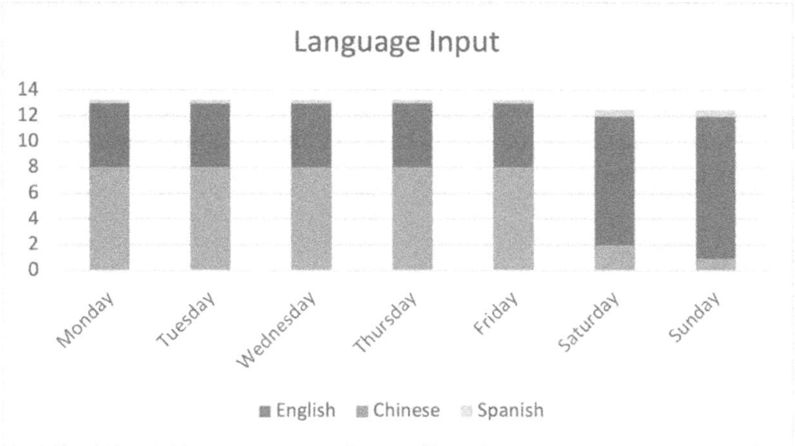

FIGURE 5.5 Language Input

plan for the children's trilingual development. Ideally, children need to learn languages as functions of everyday life at home and in educational settings.

Recognizing the influence of the cultural contexts and continuous practices for language learning, CoCo and I sought out additional Spanish-learning opportunities within our community. For example, we borrowed more picture books representing Spanish-speaking countries from the library, purchased more bilingual books, and borrowed a Spanish learning textbook from a teacher friend. When CoCo learned new subjects in her Spanish class, we searched for relevant videos online and watched them in Spanish. Moreover, we attended local events, such as visiting the Spanish-speaking booths at the international festival and participating in the Latinx Heritage Month events. Furthermore, we attended the Spanish language conversation table at the university, where college students practiced speaking Spanish. Through these experiences, CoCo articulated the value of trilingualism, stating,

> 你会说一种，两种，三种。很好的 chance 和机会把她突破。如果突破就能跟更多人 communicate，玩，和说话，聊天。如果你只有一种语言，你就没有那么多机会看更多的人。

> [You can speak one, two, three (languages). It's a good chance and opportunity to break it through. If I did it, I could communicate, play, talk, and chat with more people. If you only have one language, you just don't have as many opportunities to meet more people.]

Multilingualism expands opportunities for communication and cultural engagement. Multilingual learners use languages for different purposes, draw upon their linguistic repertoires, and understand different cultures through translanguaging and various modes. Supporting children in their trilingual literacy journey requires commitment, structured exposure, and community collaboration. By fostering an inclusive multilingual environment, educators and families can empower multilingual children to embrace their linguistic and cultural identities and thrive in a global society.

Inquiry Questions

Questions for Researchers:

- How does a bilingual speaker learn a third language? How does a plurilingual language user learn an additional language?
- How do trilingual speakers build their linguistic and cultural identities?
- How can multilingual learners leverage their full linguistic repertoire in language learning?

Questions for Teachers:

- How can teachers value students' diverse linguistic and cultural backgrounds?
- How can teachers nurture students' intercultural awareness?
- What instructional strategies best support trilingual literacy development?

Questions for Parents:

- What could parents do to support a child's trilingual development and trilingual identity at home?
- What community resources could parents find or use to help their child(ren) learn an additional language?

Suggested Reading

Braun, A., & Cline, T. (2014). *Language strategies for trilingual families: Parents' perspectives*. Multilingual Matters.

Festman, J., Poarch, G., & Dewaele, J. (2017). *Raising multilingual children*. Multilingual Matters.Wang, X. (2008). *Growing up with three languages: Birth to eleven.* Multilingual Matters.

Wang, X. (2011). *Learning to read and write in the multilingual family*. Multilingual Matters.

6 CONCLUDING THOUGHTS

This book aims to provide teachers, researchers, educators, parents, and community members with deeper insights into the lives and literacy development of bilingual and multilingual children by examining one child in depth. In this concluding chapter, I highlight some of my thoughts and suggestions as we move forward and think more about ways to value bilingual children and their literacy development and promote bilingualism. I want to close the book by reflecting on the previous chapters and offering recommendations that we can take to support and empower bilingual and multilingual children and their literacy development at home, at school, and within the broader community.

Biliteracy Development

CoCo's literacy development in both languages evolved as an interconnected process. She utilized her full linguistic repertoire (García & Li, 2014), and her biliteracy skills were developing as a holistic system. CoCo also employed natural reading strategies in both English and Chinese languages, as well as in her third language, Spanish. Moreover, the dominant language, English, influenced her approach to the other two languages. The findings suggest that her effective reading strategies in English may or may not work in other languages due to language differences. For example, in third grade, CoCo prioritized graphophonics over context clues and prior knowledge when reading English but relied on context clues and prior knowledge to predict homophones and polyphones in Chinese.

Additionally, CoCo's bilingual reading significantly contributed to the development of her bilingual writing, aligning with previous research on bilingual

DOI: 10.4324/9781003517061-6

development (Baker, 2014). To be more specific, exposure to multigenre and multimodal texts enhanced her writing development and nurtured her identity as a writer. Her journal entries demonstrated intertextual connections, reflecting various texts that she had read over time. Through journaling practices over four years, CoCo developed both as an author and a multilingual learner.

Children's literature books, particularly multicultural and multilingual texts, served as windows, mirrors, and sliding doors for multilingual learners (Bishop, 1990). These texts provided meaningful contexts for CoCo's literacy development and served as the mentor texts for her writing development. Reading and discussing multilingual books with peers, teachers, and family members further enriched her learning experience.

Multimodality played a crucial role in CoCo's emergent literacy development journey. As discussed in Chapter 2, she engaged with picturebooks and illustrated texts, leveraging both print and visual information on the page for enhanced comprehension. Similarly, in Chapter 3, CoCo journaled in different modes—multilingual texts and her illustrations. Additionally, CoCo incorporated colored pens and pencils and even borrowed mixed media—stickers and paper cutouts in her journal entries. In Chapters 4 and 5, CoCo created many multimodal artifacts in her responses to multicultural and multilingual literature books. She even created self-portraits with both texts and drawings. By integrating multimodality, CoCo deepened her comprehension, strengthened her biliteracy skills, and cultivated her identity as a multilingual learner.

Translanguaging Practices

Multilingual children's identities are closely tied to their languages—their full linguistic repertoires (García & Li, 2014). In fact, multilingual children, like CoCo, demonstrate their linguistic talents as they redesign codes and create their own codes to convey meaning. In the reading process, translanguaging is a unique way for multilingual children to understand text in any language efficiently (García & Li, 2014). In Chapter 2, CoCo invented her hidden connectors—homophones, words with multiple translations, and combined words—for decoding and understanding. She was also accustomed to translating the text into another language for her understanding. Similar to the ways in which monolingual children paraphrase part of a text for meaning-making, multilingual learners like CoCo translate between languages for comprehension in reading and communication in real life (Baker, 2014). This shows their proficiency in both or multiple languages.

This study affirms the growing body of research that highlights translanguaging as an effective strategy for bilingual children's reading comprehension and development (Moody et al., 2021; Yang et al., 2021). Multilingual children's literature served as windows and mirrors for multilingual children, added cultural authenticity to those books, and gave natural and valuable examples of translanguaging use in real life. The findings of CoCo's bilingual reading, responses to literature books, and journal entries suggest that she possessed one holistic linguistic system, leveraging her languages for pragmatic communication. Translanguaging contributed to her meaning-making processes and fostered her confidence boost as a reader and a writer.

This investigation of CoCo's biliteracy development underscores that literacy learning should be an engaging and joyful process rather than a rigid decoding or encoding exercise using separate language systems. CoCo used her full linguistic repertoire and symbols for meaning-making. Meanwhile, her linguistic knowledge grew as she practiced her languages. Her multiliteracy development highlighted that translanguaging between different languages helped children develop their literacy skills and value various languages as they speak, listen, read, and write. These findings align with previous studies on multilingual literacy (Back et al., 2020; García, 2020; García & Schleppegrell, 2021; Hill et al., 2020; Kwon & Schallert, 2016; Rowe, 2018; Salmerón, 2022; Smith, 2020; Zheng, 2021). The previous chapters presented how CoCo's translanguaging showed her strong motivation to learn multiple languages, her greater metalinguistic awareness, linguistic consciousness, and sociolinguistic consciousness. Equally important, CoCo's translanguaging affirmed her bilingual identities and devotion to more significant social interaction, communication, and empowerment.

Identity Formation

Children's identities continuously evolve across time and social contexts, as Baker and Wright (2021) discussed. In addition to developing her literacy skills, CoCo constructed her linguistic and cultural identities through reading multilingual texts, discussing literature books with others, and writing about her life experience. As CoCo spoke two languages daily and added Spanish as her third language, she constantly made cultural connections in her literacy practices. Likewise, transnational connections occurred frequently in her reading and writing activities. CoCo's global awareness emerged along with her transnational connections and was emphasized in her Spanish learning experiences. In that way, CoCo solidified her identity as a global citizen.

This study also highlights that CoCo's emergent identity development was a family investment in her languages and cultures (Darvin & Norton, 2015; Norton, 2013, 2018); however, other community members and situations also created and refined her identities (Baker & Wright, 2021). Her reading behaviors, responses to literature books, journal writing, third language learning, and interactions with family and community members all contributed to her negotiation of dynamic multilingual, multicultural identity development.

Home and Community

As we know, parents play a critical role in fostering children's multilingual development (Baker & Wright, 2021; Wang, 2008). This study leveraged a rich multilingual multimodal home literacy environment alongside virtual and community-based learning opportunities. Parents serve as children's first teachers and best advocates. Parents' beliefs and practices shape their children's language development and identity formation. In addition to access to bilingual and multilingual books at home, CoCo had environmental print in the house, to which I provided access. Moreover, talking about her reading and language learning was crucial because she could identify her difficulties, and I could help her uncover her strategies or share my strategies in the moment with her.

During the COVID-19 pandemic, home context and family literacy practice became even more significant when children had virtual school. The reading and writing practices at home supported CoCo's literacy development of her heritage language and English. Likewise, the virtual communities helped her connect with children and families of similar backgrounds and provided a new space for learning a third language beyond traditional school settings. Those spaces beyond the home and school expanded her learning experiences and provided real contexts for her multilingual development. Indeed, home and community spaces shared in the previous chapters disrupted the monolingual practices for multilingual children like CoCo. Those spaces created the tension between home and school, where two languages were spoken and two cultures were represented. Building the literacy practices that connected those spaces helped CoCo develop her biliteracy and form her identity. Schools and communities must work collaboratively to disrupt monolingual norms and create inclusive environments where multilingual learners thrive.

Challenges and Limitations

As a family raising a trilingual child, we have experienced many unique challenges over the past few years. For example, the world language program of our school district did not offer a Chinese language course at our zoned schools. Therefore, CoCo attended kindergarten at an English and Mandarin Chinese bilingual immersion school 20 miles away, approximately 40 minutes driving for a single trip. Unfortunately, she stayed for only a few months and had to switch to virtual learning due to the COVID-19 pandemic. Following that, CoCo attended a district-wide English-only virtual school for two years. At that time, she had limited access to diverse books and multilingual resources in her first-grade and second-grade virtual classes. When CoCo eventually returned to a physical third-grade monolingual classroom, the student population at her school was not diverse, with approximately 19% of students of color, and there were only two Asian American children in her classroom out of 20 students. Although the school and teachers initiated limited events and activities for multilingual students, they were open to and welcomed ideas from CoCo and me for sharing Chinese festivals, holding Chinese language and culture club, and leading Kung Fu club for the students.

This study primarily focused on the home context and limited community resources during the COVID-19 pandemic, leaving gaps in understanding how bilingual learners navigate monolingual school environments. It is certainly important to study how to disrupt the monolingual practice in the general education classroom and in the larger community. Moreover, children need a multi-dimensional environment to build their identities. For this reason, a limitation of this study is that school observation and assessment data were not included.

Although raciolinguistics and social justice were not focused on in the analysis and discussion due to the purpose of this book and the data collected, CoCo's encounters with these subjects emerged from her school and community involvement. For instance, one child in the kindergarten commented on CoCo's different skin color and said, "You don't belong here." Another child in third grade assumed that CoCo was born in China and came from there because she spoke Chinese language and shared Chinese culture with other students at school. I had multiple conversations with CoCo to clear her confusion and talk about her identity as a bilingual Chinese American. The AsianCrit framework could be employed in bilingual education and mainstream classrooms to value Asian/Asian American children's cultural and linguistic diversity and help with their identity formation (Tian et al., 2024). Further research should explore strategies to integrate bilingual education within mainstream classrooms and address systemic barriers faced by multilingual learners.

As a parent researcher and bilingual educator, I was fortunate to have the knowledge and skills to teach my child and observe her biliteracy development. However, many parents and families may not have the knowledge and resources that we have access to. Also, the strategies that we adopted for CoCo's bilingual development may not fit other children's language development and other families' language policy preferences. There is no standardized bilingual developmental path for different children.

I attempted to balance CoCo's language input and ensure she was immersed in an environment that enabled her to acquire her heritage language when she was little. In this book, CoCo developed Chinese and English simultaneously. However, multilingual children learn languages differently, so there is no particular order in which languages must be learned. With CoCo learning more and more academic English at school and in the monolingual-speaking community, keeping her heritage language and developing it as rigorously as the English language was challenging and will continue to be a challenge. Furthermore, although maintaining handwriting promotes the perception of visual word forms (Guan et al., 2021), learning to handwrite Chinese characters is time-consuming and requires practice. Moreover, we may also face other challenges that many other immigrant families reported (Liang & Shin, 2021; Meacham et al., 2025), for instance, lack of time and energy, and difficulty in maintaining motivation for learning the heritage language and the third language.

Implications and Opportunities

Research

The findings of this study have a number of research implications. This study informs researchers on conducting longitudinal ethnographic case studies with bilingual or multilingual families. In particular, it will hopefully draw more parent researchers to study their children's bilingual and multilingual development from an insider's perspective and with close observations. Also, longitudinal studies following bilingual and multilingual children in different real-life and virtual contexts, such as school, family, and community, and even across countries, would provide more implications for bilingual and trilingual literacy development.

Further research could also be conducted to investigate family commitment in bilingual children's reading and writing practices and parents' engagement to support bilingual children's identity development. Further research can explore bilingual and multilingual families' impacts on children's linguistic and cultural identities, bicultural families' responses to culturally relevant and sustaining literature books, and bilingual children's designing and redesigning of multimodal artifacts for their identity representations. Last, further studies should examine how multilingual families challenge the monolingual norms and leverage families in their children's literacy development and identity investment.

Considerably more work will need to be done to explore questions like: What are the tensions between home and school and between home and community for multilingual children? How do we build connections between those spaces? How can we build intersections between different languages and cultures for multilingual children so they can achieve and excel?

Teaching

This study suggests some important implications for future practice. Knowing the bilingual and multilingual development process can help educators and teachers bridge the differences between multiple languages and help bilingual and multilingual users achieve academic success. Recognizing that bilingual development is not a one-size-fits-all process, teachers should observe children closely and adopt responsive pedagogical approaches that value students. These findings suggest that kidwatching (Goodman & Owocki, 2002) and reading conferences with multilingual children and their families provide beneficial information for teaching more than just curriculum-based and standardized test scores. Educators can also use children's funds of knowledge (González et al., 2005; Moll, 2014) and multimodal funds of knowledge (Brown & Zhang, 2024) and help children build connections to their real lives.

Another important practical implication is that teachers should allow multilingual children to use their full linguistic repertoires, talk about their "hidden connectors" as in Chapter 2, and value their unique ways of meaning-making. Teachers can build a multilingual reading and writing workshop, encourage children to read and write in multiple languages, and use the languages that they prefer. Teachers can also encourage multilingual children to use different modes to design their products. Continued efforts are needed for teachers to create more translanguaging spaces, expose emergent multilingual speakers to multiple languages, and enhance multilingual children's meaning-making.

There is, therefore, a definite need for literacy and language educators to communicate and collaborate with parents to support young children's bilingual and bicultural development at home and at school. Teachers can recommend the literacy practices that CoCo and I did in the previous four chapters to multilingual families and suggest multicultural and multilingual children's literature books. When working with bilingual families and communities, language teachers and researchers can encourage their use of full linguistic repertoires to make meaning and recommend that parents provide a rich multimodal home literacy environment using found objects and loose parts.

Family

Setting up the family language policy is not difficult; however, maintaining these language practices requires intentional effort from families. Only having the family language policy of speaking the heritage language at home is not enough. A reasonable approach to tackle this issue could be to help parents understand that raising bilingual and multilingual children takes time and commitment. Moreover, it takes the whole village to raise multilingual learners and cultivate global citizens. Community engagement, cultural events, and language immersion opportunities further reinforce multilingualism as a lifelong asset. Parents and community partners can help provide a bilingual environment and access to multilingual resources, for example, with environmental text, resources, and events. Parents and community partners can also create more spaces and opportunities for multilingual children to read, write, and create with their languages.

No matter what languages the children use, meaning-making should be the center of literacy practices.

Parents can purposefully adopt more heritage languages in their conversations, which would help children acquire and practice those languages. Parents need to understand that children employ their full linguistic repertoires and remain flexible with their children's language uses. Equally important, parents and community partners need to better support children's multilingual development, providing more resources and spaces for children to gain interest in speaking more languages and continue learning them. Likewise, to develop a third language, a family would need a dynamic family language plan for the children. Ideally, children need to learn all languages as functions of everyday life at home, at school, and in the community.

Taken together, parents need to create spaces, initiate language use activities, and advocate for their multilingual children. In this study, our writing table was the dining table where the three of us spent the most family time (see Figures 1.4, 3.4, and 4.4). We had our meals, teatime, game time, video chatting time with friends, writing journals, doing artwork and crafts, and video conferencing for tons of lessons around the roundtable. We spent most of our family time at the table in the house. The table carried learning moments, reflections, and family memories.

Final Words

Language learning is not an isolated process, especially for children who grow up in multilingual, multicultural contexts. Children use their own linguistic repertoires, which means Chinese, English, and Spanish for CoCo in this book. The two languages in bilingual development have a symbiotic relationship for emergent bilingual children. That is to say, the two languages depend on each other to coexist and live. Bilingual speakers develop two languages, just like using a pair of chopsticks to grasp food. Each single stick is a language, and they must work together for children to acquire their knowledge, understand the culture, and perceive the global context. The two sticks look like they are parallel, but they must cross to pick up food. The two sticks could look different, but they are inseparable, and we need to use a pair to support each other. Similarly, bilingualism thrives when languages coexist and support one another. As CoCo shared in an interview,

> 我想跟大家说非常 important 的 lesson。如果能坚持，一直相信自己，就会更成功。
> [I want to tell everyone a very important lesson. If you can persist and always believe in yourself, (you) will become more successful.]

CoCo's Note

After reading my manuscripts, CoCo drafted a reflection of her language learning experiences as below.

I am CoCo in this book. My official name is Shiyang Carol Li. I am 10 years old and in fifth grade. Before I was born, my parents were in Columbia, Missouri, and I was born in Columbia, South Carolina. The two Cs are capitalized because they represent the two different Columbias. My parents are originally from China, so I am an American-born Chinese. I hope you enjoyed reading this book about me and my language learning experiences. I would like to share some of my thoughts in this note.

My Language Learning Journey

Being a trilingual learner to me means that I know three languages, and they all matter. I have different reasons for learning each language. Since my parents are from Mainland China, and my relatives live there, it is necessary for me to use Chinese so I can communicate with them. I went back to China three times after the pandemic, and I learned some interesting dialects from different parts of China, for example, Dalian, Hangzhou, and Sichuan dialects. My mom taught me Chinese using Chinese textbooks that are from Mainland China. Whenever I talk to other people who speak Chinese in the U.S., they always think I am from China, and they compliment me for speaking the language like a native speaker. I felt wonderful to be complimented. At the same time, I thought all of my time and effort of learning Chinese has been paid off.

English is very necessary for school and living in the U.S. I learn English mostly at school. We do different practices, such as reading different types of books, answering questions from the text, and writing about different topics. We use online websites such as Epic and Learning Ally, and we also spend 20 minutes each day on Progress Learning, either on math or ELA. At home, I read books, learn new words, and write in my diary.

My reason for learning Spanish is that in the future, I want to go somewhere where people speak Spanish, like Ecuador, Spain, Mexico, etc., and it would be cool and proud to learn an additional language. I used to learn Spanish as a world language class at my elementary school, but now it is one of the exploratory classes that students can choose at my intermediate school. I do not take the elective Spanish class anymore because the information that the teacher teaches is not enough for me. Instead, I started learning more Spanish using Duolingo a couple of years ago and just hit a huge milestone of 1000 days of practice! I also began with a Spanish tutor this year. We meet once a week, and she teaches me more complicated Spanish words, tenses, verbs, etc. I think that Duolingo is helpful, but I learn more things with a tutor. This is because I can learn more things that I am weak at with my Spanish tutor. I can also ask questions about things I am confused about right away and get the answer. Now, my Spanish level is about intermediate from Duolingo, and I can even talk to the waiter in Spanish when my family and I go to a Mexican restaurant!

I was motivated to learn the languages through reading. I had books in Chinese and English in my home library, and sometimes I went to the public library to get Spanish books to read. I also brought books on the car to read when we were on a trip. Pronouncing Chinese pinyin was sometimes challenging for me because I mixed up some letters with their sounds in English. The tone marks were confusing for me at the beginning. But now, I understand more about the tone marks.

I also learn languages through writing. Writing is an action of creating something with your pencil or computer. There are different types of writing, and each of them provides different types of useful information to other people. At school, we do writing, like answering questions from the text, writing about certain topics, or free writing. We also do narrative writing, persuasive writing, informational writing, biography writing, poems, etc. I wrote in a mix of pictures, Chinese, and English in my diary. I wrote a variety of different topics. We had a celebration every hundred days. This kept me writing for a long time. Sometimes, I shared my diary with my family members, and I felt proud because I had written it and shared my true thoughts. Sometimes, I wrote short pieces and drew pictures that went along with them. The challenge of writing is that sometimes I cannot write clearly about what I want to talk about, or I do not know what words to use that match my topic.

Fun Stories

There are some interesting stories about me learning languages and cultures. When I was little, my mom asked me if I had done my chores for the day. I proudly announced in English, "Mail!" But my mom was very surprised, saying, "Why are you proud of yourself when you did nothing?" Then, I repeated myself and explained that I went to get the mail from the mailbox. It turned out that she thought I said "没有 méi yǒu" in Chinese, which sounds very similar to "mail" but means "no" in English.

When I was practicing Spanish on Duolingo, one question was, "What is *Graciosa* in English?" Since I knew that a lot of Spanish words and English words looked and sounded similar, I guessed the answer and typed, *Graceful* because they look alike. But I was wrong. The correct answer turned out to be *Funny*.

I like sharing what I know about different languages. I taught English to my jiù mā, the wife of my uncle, when I went to China. I taught her English words like the alphabet, colors, numbers, etc. My cousins learned English at school.

Sometimes, they shared with me what they learned. In the U.S., I frequently video chat with my lǎolao, and sometimes I teach her some English. At school, I taught Chinese to some of my friends during recess. My Chinese American friend and I had plans for what to teach our American friends. Our "students" were very interested in Chinese and the culture, so we taught them whatever they wanted to learn. We frequently did one-to-one practices and tested them on what we taught.

I also learned Korean from a friend in fourth grade at school. She was born in South Korea and knew some Korean. Usually, we taught each other during lunch or recess. We even created our own secret "code," which was a mix of Korean and Chinese. For example, one of the codes that we made was "Nino," which meant "Hello." This code comes from "nǐ hǎo" (meaning hello) in Chinese and "ano" (The correct spelling is annyeong, meaning hello) in Korean. When we did an All About Me project in class, we both wrote in English first. Following that, I added Chinese words to my introduction, and she added Korean to hers. Then, I added Chinese words to her introduction, and she added Korean to mine. Our teacher said that it was very creative and showed a good example of language use. The two of us also made a picture book about two Asian American girls' friendship and a fictional novel about a Chinese girl immigrating to the U.S. and adjusting to her school life. We included Asian culture in both books.

Another friend is mixed race and speaks Spanish. One time, she and I did a cultural exchange. I gave her one of my Chinese vanilla creamy rabbit candies, and she gave me one of her Mexican strawberry chewy jelly Mentos. Both of these candies are very popular in each of our cultures, and we got to share the candies and our culture with each other.

Difficult Experiences

Even though I have positive experiences, I also have unpleasant school experiences. In third grade, my Chinese American friend and I were bullied because we were wearing masks. During recess time, a kid walked up to us and asked, "Why are you wearing a weird looking mask? Are you just afraid that you are going to get the virus that was literally caused by yourself???" That kid teased us several times after that because the two of us were wearing masks, and we were Chinese American. I felt mad and frustrated as we walked away. We were just trying to protect ourselves and stay safe from the virus!

Also, I feel frustrated whenever I type my name on the computer. This is because it immediately pops up the red grammar mistake line, indicating my spelling is wrong, but it is not. At the beginning of my fifth grade at the intermediate school, when my teacher said my full name, some children whispered, "Is that even a name?" "What name is that?" and "What a weird name!" I thought, "You don't have the power to judge me!" My inner spirit was like fire, bubbling up into a volcanic eruption. But I told myself to control my feelings, and not let their mean words make me unhappy.

Suggestions

Lastly, I have some suggestions for teachers. First, the district and schools can provide more languages as elective classes because students should have the choice to learn whatever language they want to or are interested in. Also, teachers can make learning fun, like making games, crafts, and other fun activities. Some activities include talking, communicating, and writing in both languages, writing small pieces, making books, drawing using different media, designing projects that are related to different cultures, etc. Teachers can also create classroom leaderboards. Teachers should always encourage students to use the languages that they are learning. My previous teachers allowed me to share different Chinese festivals with my class, and it made me feel very comfortable. All my teachers did "All About Me" projects at the beginning of the school year, and one of them let students share with one another so we could know each other better. I included my name and culture in my project and shared it with others. I thank all of my teachers for teaching and encouraging me.

I want to share with all the children: Never give up when it is hard because learning is always a process. Practice, practice, and practice. If you want to learn another language, you can use a website like Duolingo, create a handy small notebook to write what you learned, and learn with a private tutor. Keep a goal and work hard to accomplish it. This year, I want to be able to write a full paragraph in Spanish all by myself. In the future of my Spanish learning journey, I also want to be able to communicate in Spanish with ease. In the future of my life, I hope to write a story in English. Lastly, I want to teach other people Chinese. It is never too late to learn, read, and write in a new language, as well as knowing its culture. We can do amazing things together!

Shiyang Li 李师杨
February 28, 2025

REFERENCES

Back, M., Han, M., & Weng, S. C. (2020). Emotional scaffolding for emergent multilingual learners through translanguaging: Case stories. *Language and Education, 34*(5), 387–406. https://doi.org/10.1080/09500782.2020.1744638

Baker, C. (2014). *A parents' and teachers' guide to bilingualism* (4th ed.). Multilingual Matters.

Baker, C., & Wright, W. E. (2021). *Foundations of bilingual education and bilingualism* (7th ed.). Multilingual Matters.

Bishop, R. S. (1990). Mirrors, windows, and sliding glass doors. *Perspectives: Choosing and Using Books for the Classroom*, *6*(3), ix–xi.

Braun, A., & Cline, T. (2014). *Language strategies for trilingual families: Parents' perspectives*. Multilingual Matters.

Brown, S. (2016). Story nights: An apprenticeship into literacy through bilingual story reading. *Teaching Education*, *27*(3), 286–304. https://doi.org/10.1080/10476210.2016.1143459

Brown, S. (2021). Emergent bilinguals as text designers: Rendering meaning through signs. *English Teaching: Practice and Critique*, *20*(2), 130–148. https://doi.org/10.1108/ETPC-07-2020-0076

Brown, S., & Hao, L. (2022). *Multimodal literacies in young emergent bilinguals: Beyond print-centric practices*. Multilingual Matters.

Brown, S., & Zhang, R. (2024). *Multimodal funds of knowledge in literacy: Countering deficit narratives of diverse families.* Taylor & Francis.

Canagarajah, S. (2011). Codemeshing in academic writing: Identifying teachable strategies of translanguaging. *The Modern Language Journal, 95*(3), 401–417. https://doi.org/10.1111/j.1540-4781.2011.01207.x

Columbia, South Carolina Population. (2023, May). World population review. Retrieved July 3, 2025, from https://worldpopulationreview.com/us-cities/south-carolina/columbia

Compton-Lilly, C. (2021). Turtles, tortoises, ethnographies, and case study: Nuances of difference and design. In M. H. Mallette & N. K. Duke (Eds.), *Literacy research methodologies* (3rd ed., pp. 7–26). The Guilford Press.

Compton-Lilly, C., Kim, J., Quast, E., Tran, S., & Shedrow, S. (2019). The emergence of transnational awareness among children in immigrant families. *Journal of Early Childhood Literacy, 19*(1), 3–33. https://doi.org/10.1177/1468798417696342

Cowan, K., & Kress, G. (2017). Documenting and transferring meaning in the multimodal world: Reconsidering "transcription." In F. Serafini & E. Gee (Eds.), *Remixing multiliteracies: Theory and practice from New London to new times* (pp. 50–61). Teachers College Press.

Creswell, J. W., & Creswell, J. D. (2018). *Research design: Qualitative, quantitative, and mixed methods approaches*. Sage.

Crisfield, E. (2021). *Bilingual families: A practical language planning guide.* Multilingual Matters.

Cunningham, U. (2020). *Growing up with two languages: A practical guide for multilingual families and those who support them* (4th ed.). Routledge.

Daniel, S. M., & Pacheco, M. B. (2016). Translanguaging practices and perspectives of four multilingual teens. *Journal of Adolescent & Adult Literacy, 59*(6), 653–663. https://doi.org/10.1002/jaal.500

Darvin, R., & Norton, B. (2015). Identity and a model of investment in applied linguistics. *Annual Review of Applied Linguistics, 35*, 36–56. https://doi.org/10.1017/S0267190514000191

Davenport, M. R. (2002). *Miscues not mistakes: Reading assessment in the classroom.* Heinemann.

Dietrich, S., & Hernandez, E. (2022, August). *Language use in the United States: 2019.* U.S. Census Bureau. https://www.census.gov/content/dam/Census/library/publications/2022/acs/acs-50.pdf

Espinosa, C. M., & Ascenzi-Moreno, L. (2021). *Rooted in strength: Using translanguaging to grow multilingual readers and writers.* Scholastic.

Esteban, M., & Moll, L. (2014). Funds of identity: A new concept based on the Funds of Knowledge approach. *Culture & Psychology, 20*(1), 31–48. https://doi.org/10.1177/1354067X13515934

Fisher, D., & Frey, N. (2013). *Better learning through structured teaching: A framework for the gradual release of responsibility* (2nd ed.). ASCD.

Franck, J., Faloppa, F., & Marinis, T. (2024). *Myths and facts about multilingualism.* CALEC-TBR Books.

Fu, D., Hadjioannou, X., & Zhou, X. (2019). *Translanguaging for emergent bilinguals: Inclusive teaching in the linguistically diverse classroom.* Teacher College Press.

García, O. (2017). Translanguaging in schools: Subiendo y bajando, bajano y subiendo as afterward. *Journal of Language, Identity, and Education, 16*(4), 256–263. https://doi.org/10.1080/15348458.2017.1329657

García, O. (2020). Translanguaging and Latinx bilingual readers. *The Reading Teacher, 73*(5), 557–562. https://doi.org/10.1002/trtr.1883

García, O., Johnson, S. I., Seltzer, K., & Valdés, G. (2017). *The translanguaging classroom: Leveraging student bilingualism for learning*. Caslon.

García, O., & Li, W. (2014). *Translanguaging: Language, bilingualism and education.* Palgrave Macmillan. https://doi.org/10.1057/9781137385765

Garcia, M, H., & Schleppegrell, M. J. (2021). Culturally sustaining disciplinary literacy for bi/multilingual learners: Creating a translanguaging social studies classroom. *Journal of Adolescent & Adult Literacy, 64*(4), 449–454. https://doi.org/10.1002/jaal.1129

Gee, J. P. (2014). *How to do discourse analysis: A toolkit*. Routledge.

Glazier, J., & Seo, J. A. (2011). Multicultural literature and discussion as mirror and window? *Journal of Adolescent & Adult Literacy, 48*(8), 686–700. https://doi.org/10.1598/JAAL.48.8.6

González, N., Moll, L. C., & Amanti, C. (2005). *Funds of knowledge: Theorizing practices in households, communities, and classrooms*. Routledge.

Goodman, K. (1973). Miscues: Windows on the reading process. In K. Goodman (Ed.), *Miscue analysis: Applications to reading instruction* (pp. 3–14). NCTE.

Goodman, K. (2014). Reading, writing, and written texts: A transactional sociopsycholinguistic view. In K. S. Goodman & Y. M. Goodman (Eds.), *Making sense of learners making sense of written language: The selected works of Kenneth S. Goodman and Yetta M. Goodman* (pp. 43–55). Routledge. https://doi.org/10.4324/9780203366929

Goodman, Y. (1978). Kidwatching: An alternative to testing. *The National Elementary Principal, 57*(4), 41–45.

Goodman, K., Fries, P. H., & Strauss, S. L. (2016). *Reading—the grand illusion: How and why people make sense of print.* Erlbaum.

Goodman, K., Wang, S., Iventosch, M. S., & Goodman, Y. (2012). *Reading in Asian languages: Making sense of written texts in Chinese, Japanese, and Korean.* Routledge.

Goodman, Y., Martens, P., & Flurkey, A. D. (2014). *The essential RMA: A window into readers' thinking.* Richard C. Owen.

Goodman, Y., & Owocki, G. (2002). *Kidwatching: Documenting children's literacy development*. Heinemann.

Goodman, Y., Watson, D. J., & Burke, C. L. (2005). *Reading miscue inventory: From evaluation to instruction* (2nd ed.). Richard C. Owen.

Gration, E. (2023, October 13). *Bilingualism in 2023: US, UK & Global Statistics.* Preply.

Guan, C. Q., Smolen, E. R., Meng, W., & Booth, J. R. (2021). Effect of handwriting on visual word recognition in Chinese bilingual children and adults. *Frontiers in Psychology, 12*, 1–12. https://doi.org/10.3389/fpsyg.2021.628160

Halliday, M. A. K. (1982). Three aspects of children's language development: Learning language, learning through language, learning about language. In Y. Goodman, M. Haussler, & D. Strickland (Eds.), *Oral and written language development research: Impact on the schools* (pp. 1–27). NCTE.

Hao, L. (2023). Reading global literature with Chinese American children: Connections, disconnections, and misconnections. *Talking Points, 35*(1), 11–18. https://doi.org/10.58680/tp202332706

Hao, L. (2024). Uplifting the voices of Asian American parents through an online family book club: Elicited and silenced cultural knowledge. *Literacy Research: Theory, Method, and Practice, 73*(1), 126–149. https://doi.org/10.1177/23813377241285839

Hao, L., & Wang, Y. (2022). A new way of empowering an English learning family: Virtual Family Miscue Analysis. *Multicultural Education, 29*(3–4), 26–33.

Hill, K., Ponder, J. M., Summerlin, J., & Evans, P. (2020). Two language books: The power and possibilities of leveraging multilingual texts for critical translanguaging pedagogy. *Journal of Higher Education Theory & Practice, 20*(12), 197–209. https://doi.org/10.33423/jhetp.v20i12.3791

Hipfner-Boucher, K., Lam, K., & Chen, X. (2014). The effects of bilingual education on the English language and literacy outcomes of Chinese-speaking children. *Written Language & Literacy*, *17*(1), 116–138. https://doi.org/10.1075/wll.17.1.06hip

Janks, H., Dixon, K., Ferreira, A., Granville, S., & Newfield, D. (2013). *Doing critical literacy: Texts and activities for students and teachers*. Routledge.

Jewitt, C. (2008). Multimodality and literacy in school classrooms. *Review of Research in Education*, *32*(1), 241–267. https://doi.org/10.3102/0091732X07310586

Kabuto, B. (2010). *Becoming biliterate: Identity, ideology, and learning to read and write in two languages*. Routledge.

Kabuto, B. (2017). A socio-psycholinguistic perspective on biliteracy: The use of miscue analysis as a culturally relevant assessment tool. *Reading Horizons: A Journal of Literacy and Language Arts*, *56*(1), 25–44. Retrieved from https://scholarworks.wmich.edu/reading_horizons/vol56/iss1/2

Kabuto, B. (2022). *Becoming bilingual readers: Identity, translanguaging, and biographic biliteracy profiles*. Routledge.

Kabuto, B., & Martens, P. (Eds.). (2014). *Linking families, learning, and schooling: Parent-researcher perspective*. Routledge.

Kenner, C. (2003). Embodied knowledges: Young children's engagement with the act of writing. In C. Jewitt & G. Kress (Eds.), *Multimodal literacy* (pp. 88–106). Peter Lang.

Kim, S., & Song, K. H. (2019). Designing a community translanguaging space within a family literacy project. *The Reading Teacher*, *73*(3), 267–279. https://doi.org/10.1002/trtr.1820

Kress, G. R. (2010). *Multimodality: A social semiotic approach to contemporary communication*. Taylor & Francis.

Kress, G. R. (2011). "Partnerships in research": Multimodality and ethnography. *Qualitative Research*, *11*(3), 239–260. https://doi.org/10.1177/1468794111399836

Kress, G., & van Leeuwen, T. (2001). *Multimodal discourse: The modes and media of contemporary communication*. Oxford University Press.

Kwon, H. J., & Schallert, D. L. (2016). Understanding translanguaging practices through a biliteracy continua framework: Adult biliterates reading academic texts in their two languages. *Bilingual Research Journal*, *39*(2), 138–151. https://doi.org/10.1080/15235882.2016.1167139

Ladson-Billings, G. (2021). *Culturally relevant pedagogy: Asking a different question*. Teachers College Press.

Lam, K., Chen, X., & Cummins, J. (2015). To gain or to lose: Students' English and Chinese literacy achievement in a Mandarin language bilingual program. *Canadian Journal of Applied Linguistics*, *18*(2), 96–124. Retrieved from https://journals.lib.unb.ca/index.php/CJAL/article/view/22427

Laman, T. T. (2013). *From ideas to words: Writing strategies for English language learners*. Heinemann.

Li, G. (2006). Biliteracy and trilingual practices in the home context: Case studies of Chinese-Canadian children. *Journal of Early Childhood Literacy*, *6*(3), 355–381. https://doi.org/10.1177/1468798406069797

Li, W. (2014). Who's teaching whom? Co-learning in multilingual classrooms. In S. May (Ed.), *The multilingual turn: Implications for SLA, TESOL, and bilingual education* (pp. 167–190). Routledge.

Li, W. (2018). Translanguaging as a practical theory of language. *Applied Linguistics, 39*(1), 9–30. https://doi.org/10.1093/applin/amx039

Li, X., Huang, L., Yao, P., & Hyönä, J. (2022). Universal and specific reading mechanisms across different writing systems. *Nature Reviews Psychology, 1*(3), 133–144. https://doi.org/10.1038/s44159-022-00022-6

Liang, F., & Shin, D. S. (2021). Heritage language maintenance of Chinese immigrant families: Perceptions, practices, and challenges. *Bilingual Research Journal, 44*(1), 23–38. https://doi.org/10.1080/15235882.2021.1922539

Little, S. (2020). Whose heritage? What inheritance?: Conceptualising family language identities. *International Journal of Bilingual Education and Bilingualism, 23*(2), 198–212. https://doi.org/10.1080/13670050.2017.1348463

Louie, B., & Davis-Welton, K. (2016). Family literacy project: Bilingual picture books by English learners. *The Reading Teacher, 69*(6), 597–606. https://doi.org/10.1002/trtr.1444

Macalister, J. (2017). Beginnings. In J. Macalister & S. H. Mirvahedi (Eds.), *Family language policies in a multilingual world: Opportunities, challenges, and consequences* (pp. 1–10). Routledge.

Mango Languages (n.d.). *Mango languages*. https://mangolanguages.com/

Martens, P. (1996). *I already know how to read: A child's view of literacy*. Heinemann.

Meacham, S. S., Wee, S., Kim, J., Han, S., & Hsieh, W. (2025). *Early childhood and the Asian American experience: Exploring intersectionality and addressing misrepresentations*. Routledge.

Merriam, S. B. (2009). *Qualitative research: A guide to design and implementation*. Jossey-Bass.

Miles, M. B., Huberman, A. M., & Saldaña, J. (2020). *Qualitative data analysis: A methods sourcebook* (4th ed.). Sage.

Mills, H., & Stephens, D. (2004). Theory in practice: The legacy of Louise Rosenblatt. *Language Arts, 82*(1), 47–55.

Ministry of Education of the People's Republic of China (MOE of P.R.C.) (2022). *Chinese language arts curriculum standards*. https://www.moe.gov.cn/srcsite/A26/s8001/202204/W020220420582344386456.pdf

Moll, L. (2014). *L. S: Vygotsky and education*. Routledge.

Moll, L., Amanti, C., Neff, D., & Gonzalez, N. (1992). Funds of knowledge for teaching: Using a qualitative approach to connect homes and classrooms. *Theory Into Practice, 31*(2), 132–141. https://doi.org/10.1080/00405849209543534

Moody, S. M., Matthews, S. D., & Eslami, Z. R. (2021). Translanguaging during shared read alouds: A case study. *Literacy Research and Instruction, 61*(2), 113–136. https://doi.org/10.1080/19388071.2021.1889724

Moore, R., & Gilles, C. (2005). *Reading conversations: Retrospective miscue analysis with struggling readers*. Heinemann.

Musanti, S. I., & Rodríguez, A. D. (2017). Translanguaging in bilingual teacher preparation: Exploring pre-service bilingual teachers' academic writing. *Bilingual Research Journal, 40*(1), 38–54. https://doi.org/10.1080/15235882.2016.1276028

New London Group. (1996). A pedagogy of multiliteracies: Designing social futures. *Harvard Educational Review, 66*(1), 60–92. https://doi.org/10.17763/haer.66.1.17370n67v22j160u

Newman, B. M. (2012). Mentor texts and funds of knowledge: Situating writing within our students' worlds. *Voices From the Middle*, *20*(1), 25–30. https://doi.org/10.58680/vm201220695

Noguerón-Liu, S., Shimek, C. H., & Bahlmann Bollinger, C. (2020). 'Dime De Que Se Trató/Tell me what it was about': Exploring emergent bilinguals' linguistic resources in reading assessments with parent participation. *Journal of Early Childhood Literacy*, *20*(2), 411–433. https://doi.org/10.1177/1468798418770708

Norton, B. (2013). *Identity and language learning: Extending the conversation* (2nd ed.). Multilingual Matters.

Norton, B. (2018). Identity and investment in multilingual classrooms. In A. Bonnet & P. Siemund (Eds.), *Foreign language education in multilingual classrooms* (pp. 237–252). John Benjamins.

O'Connor, C., & Joffe, H. (2020). Intercoder reliability in qualitative research: Debates and practical guidelines. *International Journal of Qualitative Methods, 19*, 1–13. https://doi.org/10.1177/1609406919899220

Osorio, S. L. (2018). Multicultural literature as a classroom tool. *Multicultural Perspectives*, *20*(1), 47–52. https://doi.org/10.1080/15210960.2018.1408348

Pan, H., & Feng, Y. (2017, March 29). Chinese semantics. In *Oxford research encyclopedia of linguistics*. Retrieved from https://doi.org/10.1093/acrefore/9780199384655.013.170.

Paugh, P., & MacPhee, D. (2023). *Learning to be literate*. Norton Professional Books.

Perry, N. J., Kay, S. M., & Brown, A. (2008). Continuity and change in home literacy practices of Hispanic families with preschool children. *Early Child Development and Care*, *178*(1), 99–113. https://doi.org/10.1080/03004430701482191

Pressley, T., Allington, R. L., & Pressley, M. (2023). *Reading instruction that works: The case for balanced teaching*. Guilford Publications.

Pu, C. (2010). The influence of heritage language and public schools on Chinese American children's biliteracy development. *Bilingual Research Journal*, *33*(2), 150–172. https://doi.org/10.1080/15235882.2010.503459

Rosenblatt, L. M. (1978/1994). *The reader, the text, the poem*. Southern Illinois University Press.

Rosenblatt, L. M. (2005a). From literature as exploration and the reader, the text, the poem. *Voices from the Middle*, *12*(3), 25–30.

Rosenblatt, L. M. (2005b). Literature – S.O.S.! *Voices from the Middle, 12*(3), 34–38.

Rosenblatt, L. M. (2018). The transactional theory of reading and writing. In D. E. Alvermann, N. J. Unrau, M. Sailors, & R. B. Ruddell (Eds.), *Theoretical models and process of literacy* (pp. 451–479). Routledge. https://doi.org/10.4324/9781315110592

Rowe, L. W. (2018). Say it in your language: Supporting translanguaging in multilingual classes. *The Reading Teacher, 72*(1), 31–38. https://doi.org/10.1002/trtr.1673

Rubinstein-Ávila, E., Sox, A. A., Kaplan, S., & McGraw, R. (2015). Does biliteracy+ mathematical discourse= binumerate development? Language use in a middle school dual-language mathematics classroom. *Urban Education*, *50*(8), 899–937. https://doi.org/10.1177/0042085914536997

Ryan, È. (2021). The impact of home literacy on bilingual vocabulary development. *Bilingual Research Journal*, *44*(1), 108–123. https://doi.org/10.1080/15235882.2021.1905105

Salmerón, C. (2022). Leveraging translanguaging practices in an elementary poetry writing workshop. *Bilingual Research Journal, 45*(1), 82–98. https://doi.org/10.1080/15235882.2022.2061638

Serafini, F. (2015). Multimodal literacy: From theories to practices. *Language Arts, 92*(6), 412–423. https://doi.org/10.58680/la201527389

Shei, C. (2014). *Understanding the Chinese language: A comprehensive linguistic introduction*. Routledge.

Short, K. (2016). A curriculum that is intercultural. In K. Short, D. Day & J. Schroeder (Eds.), *Teaching globally: Reading the world through literature* (pp. 3–24). Stenhouse.

Siegel, M. (2006). Rereading the signs: Multimodal transformations in the field of literacy education. *Language Arts, 84*(1), 65–77. https://www.jstor.org/stable/41962165

Smith, P. (2020). The case for translanguaging in Black immigrant literacies. *Literacy Research: Theory, Method, and Practice, 69*(1), 192–210. https://doi.org/10.1177/2381336920937264

Song, K. (2016). "Okay, I will say in Korean and then in American": Translanguaging practices in bilingual homes. *Journal of Early Childhood Literacy, 16*(1), 84–106. https://doi.org/10.1177/1468798414566705

Spence, L. (2014). *Student writing: Give it a generous reading*. Information Age Publishing.

Stake, R. E. (1995). *The art of case study research.* Sage.

Taylor, D. (1983). *Family literacy: Young children learning to read and write.* Heinemann.

Tian, Z., & Shepard-Carey, L. (2020). (Re) imagining the future of translanguaging pedagogies in TESOL through teacher–researcher collaboration. *TESOL Quarterly, 54*(4), 1131– 1143. https://doi.org/10.1002/tesq.614

Tian, Z., Wong, J. W., & García, S. (2024). An urgent call to center AsianCrit in Chinese/English dual language bilingual education programs. *International Multilingual Research Journal*, 1–15. https://doi.org/10.1080/19313152.2024.2377876

United States Census Bureau. (n.d.). *American community survey*. Retrieved November 20, 2023, from https://data.census.gov/table/ACSDP5Y2019.DP02?hidePreview=true

Vygotsky, L. S. (1978). *Mind in society: The development of higher psychological processes*. Harvard University Press.

Wang, X. (2008). *Growing up with three languages: Birth to eleven.* Multilingual Matters.

Wang, Q., & Andrews, J. F. (2021). Chinese pinyin: Overview, history and use in language learning for young deaf and hard of hearing students in China. *American Annals of the Deaf, 166*(4), 446–461. https://www.jstor.org/stable/27113321

Wang, Y., & Seale, E. (2019). Helping teachers understand readers better: Using Retrospective Miscue Analysis to engage children in meaningful reading conversations. *Multicultural Education, 26*(2), 30–35.

Wang, M., & Yang, C. L. (2007). Learning to read Chinese: Cognitive consequences of cross-language and writing system differences. In K. Koda & A. Zehler (Eds.), *Learning to read across languages* (pp. 137–165). Routledge. https://doi.org/10.4324/9780203935668

Wang, Y., Guo, W., & Sui, X. (2022). A content analysis of Chinese American contemporary realistic fiction books. *The Reading Teacher*, *76*(2), 159–168. https://doi.org/10.1002/trtr.2119

Watson, D., Burke, C., & Goodman, Y. (1988). Pragmatic and linguistic systems of language. In C. Gilles et al. (Eds.), *Whole language strategies for secondary students* (pp. 3–10). Richard C. Owen.

Weaver, C. (2002). *Reading process & practice* (3rd ed.). Heinemann.

Wohlwend, K., Qu, P., Scott, J. A., & Medina, C. L. (2022). Multimodal literacies at the train table: Supporting young emergent bilinguals through play. In S. Brown & L. Hao (Eds.), *Multimodal literacies in young emergent bilinguals: Beyond print-centric practices* (pp. 17–29). Multilingual Matters.

Wood, D., Bruner, J. S., & Ross, G. (1976). The role of tutoring in problem solving. *Journal of Child Psychology and Psychiatry*, *17*, 89–100. https://doi.org/10.1111/j.1469-7610.1976.tb00381.x

Yang, S., Kiramba, L. K., & Wessels, S. (2021). Translanguaging for biliteracy: Book reading practices in a Chinese bilingual family. *Bilingual Research Journal*, *44*(1), 39–55. https://doi.org/10.1080/15235882.2021.1907486

Zheng, B. (2021). Translanguaging in a Chinese immersion classroom: An ecological examination of instructional discourses. *International Journal of Bilingual Education and Bilingualism*, *24*(9), 1324–1339. https://doi.org/10.1080/13670050.2018.1561642

Children's Literature Cited

Chapter 2

English Texts

Applegate, K. (2015). *The one and only Ivan* (P. Castelao, Illus.). Storytide.

Armed but not dangerous. (2017). In K. Hodkinson, S. Adams & E. Hodkinson, *Wordly wise 3000* (Vol.4, 4th ed., pp. 81–82). Educators Pub Svc Inc.

Bailey finds a new home. (2015). In K. Hodkinson & S. Adams, *Wordly wise 3000,* (Vol.2, 3rd ed., pp. 6–7). Educators Pub Svc Inc.

Brown, P. (2014). *My teacher is a monster* (P. Brown, Illus.). Little, Brown Books for Young Readers.

Dean, K., & Dean, J. (2015). *Pete the cat's train trip* (J. Dean, Illus.). HarperCollins.

Dean, K., & Dean, J. (2018). *Pete the cat and the cool caterpillar* (J. Dean, Illus.). HarperCollins.

DiCamillo, K. (2009). *Mercy Watson to the rescue* (C. Van Dusen, Illus.). Candlewick.

EOne. (2018). *Peppa's Chinese new year* (EOne, Illus.). Scholastic Inc.

Lin, G. (2019). *Where the mountain meets the moon* (G. Lin, Illus.). Little, Brown Books for Young Readers.

Litwin, E. (2010). *Pete the cat: I love my white shoes (*J. Dean, Illus.). HarperCollins.

May, K. (2013). *Coco: My delicious life (A branches book: Lotus lane. Vol. 2).* Scholastic Inc.

Reynolds, P. (2003). *The dot* (P. Reynolds, Illus.). Candlewick.

Vegara, M. I. S. (2017). *Audrey Hepburn (Little people, big dreams. Vol.7)* (A. Arrazola, Illus.). Frances Lincoln Children's Books.

Chinese Texts

羿射九日 Houyi Shoots Down Nine Suns. (2017). In R. Wen (Ed.), *Chinese language arts*, 2nd grade (Vol.2, pp. 108-109). People's Education Press.

Huang, D. (2018). 陶罐和铁罐 Clay pot and iron pot. In R. Wen (Ed.), *Chinese language arts*, 3rd grade (Vol.2, pp. 18–19). People's Education Press.

Niimi, N. (2018). 去年的树 The tree from last year (J. Sun, Trans.). In R. Wen (Ed.), *Chinese language arts*, 3rd grade (Vol.1, pp. 28–30). People's Education Press.

Niu, H. (2018). 父亲 、树林和鸟 Father, woods and birds. In R. Wen (Ed.), *Chinese language arts*, 3rd grade (Vol.1, pp. 91–92). People's Education Press.

Schubiger, J. (2017). 当世界年纪还小的时候 When the world is young (M. Lin, Trans.). In R. Wen (Ed.), *Chinese language arts*, 2nd grade (Vol.2, pp. 105–106). People's Education Press.

长腿的萝卜 The Turnip with Legs (2009). Dolphin Books.

Zheng, Z. (2018). 燕子The swallows. In R. Wen (Ed.), *Chinese language arts*, 3rd grade (Vol.2, pp. 4–5). People's Education Press.

Chapter 3

Mentor Texts Cited

Folman, A. (2018). *Anne Frank's diary: The graphic adaptation* (D. Polonsky, Illus.). Penguin.

Elliott, R. (2015–2020). *Owl diaries series*. Scholastic.

Xiaopipa (n.d.). *Xiaopipa magazine*. https://pipamag.org/

Chapter 4

Chinese/Chinese American Literature Cited

Bao, D. (2010). 跟着姥姥去遛弯儿 *Feast of treats for the high summer days* (M. Li, Illus.). Xinjiang Juvenile Publishing House.

Bao, D. (2021a). *端午粽米香 The Dragon Boat Festival and glutinous rice dumplings* (H. Xu, Illus.). Xinjiang Juvenile Publishing House.

Bao, D. (2021b). *奶奶的青团 Grandmother's green rice balls* (J. Zhou, Illus.). Xinjiang Juvenile Publishing House.

Blackburne, L. (2021). *I dream of popo* (J. Kuo, Illus.). Roaring Brook Press.

Hei, H. (2020). *爷爷的印章 Grandfather's stamp* (P. Zhang, Illus.). Jiangsu Fine Arts Publishing House.

Lin, G. (2001). *The ugly vegetables* (G. Lin, Illus.). Charlesbridge.

Lin, G. (2010). *Thanking the moon: Celebrating the mid-autumn festival* (G. Lin, Illus.). Knopf Books for Young Readers.

Lin, G. (2018). *The big mooncake for little star* (G. Lin, Illus.). Little, Brown Books for Young Readers.

Lo, R. (2014). *Father's Chinese opera* (R. Lo, Illus.). Sky Pony.

Murphy, M. (2020). *What I like most* (C. Zhu, Illus.). Candlewick.

Sennah, Y. (2020). *My day with Gong Gong* (E. Chen, Illus.). Annick Press.

Tang, S. (2010). *Celebrating the lantern festival* (S. Tang, Illus.). Shanghai Press.
Thong, R. (2008). *Red is a dragon: A book of colors* (G. Lin, Illus.). Chronicle.
Wang, A. (2021). *Watercress* (J. Chin, Illus.). Neal Porter Books.
Zhang, K. (2020). *Amy Wu and the patchwork dragon* (C. Chua, Illus.). Simon & Schuster.
Zhou, X. (2018). *荷花镇的早市 Morning market in lotus town* (X. Zhou, Illus.). 21st Century Publishing Group.

Chapter 5

Spanish Literature Cited

Gonzalez, M. C. (2013). *My colors, my world / Mis colores, mi mundo* (M. Gonzalez, Illus.). Lee & Low Books.
Orozco, J. (2020). *Sing with me / Canta conmigo* (S. Palacios, Illus.). Scholastic Press.
Willems, M. (2021). *Dormiré la siesta!* Hyperion Books.
Willems, M. (2015a). *Estamos en un libro.* Hyperion Books.
Willems, M. (2015b). *¡Hoy volare!* Hyperion Books.

Index

Note: **Bold** page numbers refer to tables and *italic* page numbers refer to figures.

For Product Safety Concerns and Information please contact our EU representative GPSR@taylorandfrancis.com
Taylor & Francis Verlag GmbH, Kaufingerstraße 24, 80331 München, Germany

www.ingramcontent.com/pod-product-compliance
Ingram Content Group UK Ltd.
Pitfield, Milton Keynes, MK11 3LW, UK
UKHW021958180926
475701UK00003B/82

* 9 7 8 1 0 3 2 8 1 2 5 8 8 *